Coaching Football's Special Situations

Bob O'Connor
Al Groh

COACHES CHOICE™

ISBN: 1-58518-786-0
Library of Congress Control Number: 2001098603
Cover design: Jeanne Hamilton
Book layout: Jeanne Hamilton
Front cover photo: Scott Halleran/Allsport

Coaches Choice
P.O. Box 1828
Monterey, CA 93942
www.coacheschoice.com

Dedication

To my former players, especially those who chose coaching football as a profession: Terrell, Angel, Luis, Mark, and so many others who have dedicated their lives to educating our youth through this great game.

—Bob O'Connor

To my dad—my first coach—for his dedication and caring. To my family—Anne, Michael, Ashley and Matt—for allowing me to be their head coach.

—Al Groh

Acknowledgments

We appreciate the opportunity to work with everyone at Coaches Choice. They certainly have done a real service to football coaches by working to deliver the very best books in our field.

Contents

Foreword

I have coached with Bob and I know Al. They are both intelligent, forward-thinking coaches. To my knowledge, a book of this sort has never been published before. It talks about the "game" of football and how to win. Xs and Os are fun to draw, and then to execute, but the game of football goes well beyond formations, passes, and runs.

Coaches never have enough minutes to teach their team all that is needed to be completely prepared for a game. We must therefore allocate our time to what is most important for winning the game. Strangely, many coaches don't prioritize their time to maximize their chances of winning. This book gives valuable insights into where our priorities must lie.

Without question, every coach in America, from Pop Warner to pro, will find something of value in this book. I not only recommend it, but I believe that it is one of the three or four football coaching books that every coach must have.

Tom Flores
Former NFL Head Coach
Two-time Super Bowl-winning coach

Introduction

Most coaches know of times when the team with the better fundamentals loses. Of course, fundamentals are fundamental, but they are not the whole story. The execution of assignments is essential to winning, but sometimes the team that executes better loses. The team with the most offensive yards doesn't always score the most points. Exploiting mismatches is another important part of winning a game, but probably not as important as execution. Some of these areas are covered in this book. However, the primary emphasis of the book is to look at another essential variable to winning, namely "winning the situations." Winning these situations can mean the difference between winning and losing the game.

If each set of circumstances in a game was always the same, the sport would be relatively easy to coach. If every putt on the golf course was a five-footer on a flat green, for example, everyone would be a good putter. In football, if the score was always tied, or every third down was a third-and-one, coaching would be a much simpler task. But in golf, you seldom get the same putt, and in football, you seldom encounter an identical situation: The score is different, the players are different, the weather is different, the distance-to-go is different, the defense is different, or the time remaining is different. These variables interact with each other in continuously changing situations during every game. Because of these variables, coaches can help their teams be more effective by understanding and teaching situational football.

Additionally, coaches can often affect the situations that occur in order to turn the circumstances in their favor. For example, they can reduce penalties and turnovers while increasing those of their opponents. They can increase the effectiveness of the kicking game. They can manage the clock better. As such, the coaches who most effectively teach their teams to manage these varying situations will win the most games. That's what this book is about.

The authors will apply their collective point of view to the points addressed in this book. Whether the lesson was learned in high school, college, or professional football, the lesson is a common one. "Collective mentality" is a term that will be used throughout the book to emphasize that the coach and his players must be on the same page. They must have the same concept of what is necessary to win, and then they must execute based on that concept.

This book looks at several areas that can help a team win if they're done effectively, and can cause them to lose if they're performed poorly. Therefore, the mission of this book is to help coaches recognize how to control the situations that lead to winning. Be forewarned: With far more possible game situations than can be practiced in a single day, coaches must allocate their practice time as efficiently as possible.

The fundamental approach of this book is to cover the topics from a basic to a more-advanced level. While many of the topics covered are quite basic—particularly in the kicking game chapters—some ideas presented will be new, even to many experienced coaches. For example, many of the kicking-game ideas are far too complicated to implement for youth-league football.

While attempting to keep the chapters succinct, the kicking game chapters delve more deeply into both techniques and strategy. This approach provides less-experienced coaches with a deeper understanding of both aspects of the kicking game, especially as they apply to modern-day football. As a result, about half of this book is devoted to the kicking game. Still, the kicking game is just one of the seven essential areas in which a coach can tilt the odds in his favor and increase his team's chances of winning the game.

1

A Football Game Is More than a Jousting Match

"Football is a game of inches."
"Coaching is a race against time."

Both of these coaching maxims are true. A primary concern in coaching is to gain the greatest number of inches and yards in the shortest amount of time. On the other hand, just as accurate is the reality that a football game is much more than sixty or seventy plays run during a game to test a team's execution; rather, a football game is a kaleidoscope of ever-changing situations. A team's ability to execute proper assignments and fundamentals simultaneously, while recognizing and effectively managing game situations, is what determines its performance as a total team.

"You win with defense."
"The losing team generally makes two more mistakes in the kicking game than the winner."

More truisms! It is certainly important to increase the effectiveness of defense and to win the kicking game. It's a mistake, however, to take these segments of the total game out of context. Offense is, after all, where most of a team's points are scored. The coach should see these three aspects of the game and prepare his teams to win in each area. A team concept, or collective mentality, should be developed so the players and coaches understand how to think and react in each aspect. This total team concept includes managing a complete game, with all its changing situations, to create the best opportunity to win.

All levels of football should include time for a "compete-and-win" type of practice, including one-on-one blocking or one-on-one tackling. Physical toughness is an essential part of the game. But, it is not *The Game*. To win the game, players should be prepared for every situation they are likely to encounter. They should be prepared to play intelligently. The jousting part of the game, the necessity to beat a player physically, is the essence of the game, but it is not *The Game*—just like catching a ball is not baseball, but rather an essential part of the game. Furthermore, while shooting a basket is not basketball, it is an essential aspect of the game. In the same vein, blocking or beating a block, tackling or evading a tackle, and catching a pass or making an interception are all parts of the physical aspect of the game of football. In reality, however, the game is much more complicated than these essential skill-related attributes, collectively referred to as the "joust."

In the early days of jousting, knights merely held their lances out and spurred their horses on until the crash. One of them would probably go down. As jousting became more popular, however, more perceptive knights began to look for their opponents' weaknesses. Does he hold his shield too high or too low? Does he hold his lance high or steady on his approach? Is he better with his lance, mace, or sword? As a medieval knight, any clue to an adversary's tendencies might give him a better chance to win the joust. Even if he was knocked off his horse or injured his right arm, the joust continued. The relevant point was whether he was fully prepared for all of the possibilities.

All football coaches want to find the "winning edge." To find that edge, teams must practice the things that will win when the opponent's defense stacks up against their offense, and when their defense is equal to the opponent's offense. The game has changed since the days of the flying wedge. It goes well beyond the jousting contests of blocking and tackling.

A team could be the best three-on-three team in America, with tough guys who never give up. They might know how to block and how to beat blocks. The runners might run hard. Unfortunately, three-on-three football games are not played. The game is more complicated than that. As a general rule, for example, if the defense blitzes in that three-on-three drill, the offense will lose.

Fundamentals Are Fundamental!

Walking is fundamental to running, but it isn't running. Blocking and tackling are fundamental to playing the game of football, but they are not *The Game*. On the other hand, if players can't block and tackle, they can't play the game.

Fundamentals are important at every level of football. Matt Millen, the "All Everything" linebacker, once remarked that in a game, when things weren't going right for him, he would check his stance, then his reads, and then evaluate his reactions to the opponent's plays. Yes, fundamentals are essential at every level.

Executing the Fundamentals

Effective play execution is another essential of winning in football, as it is in other sports. The double play is practiced in baseball, the basketball team practices the full-court press, and every football team practices the punt. But, does punting effectively win the game? It helps, but the game requires much more.

Football is a very complicated and interesting sport. Winning takes more than merely perfecting the fundamentals. While blocking, tackling, throwing, catching, and kicking are absolutely essential to playing the game effectively, just as having a strong forehand and backhand is essential to a tennis player, it is how well and when these skills are used that is essential to the game.

Knowing How to Execute Assignments

Being able to execute the required assignments with the appropriate fundamentals is important. Missed assignments are a major cause of losing games. Some players have the physical ability to dominate in one-on-one drills, but are unable to successfully execute their assignments in game situations. This is unacceptable to the coach who wants to put his team in the best position to win.

Motivation and Team Cohesion

Motivation and team cohesion are arguably more important in football than in any other sport. How can coaches attain both objectives? How can they foster the feeling of the importance of winning, on the field and in life?

Without question, players must be motivated. They should want to become the strongest and quickest players possible. They should want to learn the necessary fundamentals and techniques of the game so they can perform at their best. Proper motivation is a necessary factor if athletes are to perform at a high level in any sport, and football certainly requires this type of collective motivation. It is a game of the heart. As individuals and as part of a team, players must want to perform at a high level. This attitude, too, is an essential aspect of winning.

Even with an appropriate level of execution and emotion, coupled with the inspiration of the team and perspiration of the hard practices, a team may not be sufficiently prepared to win. While fundamentals and emotion are the foundations for winning, more is always necessary on the field. Successful coaches should plan for the unexpected and should practice dealing with the situations that can turn the game in their favor.

The Next Level of Coaching

All coaches realize the importance of learning the proper fundamentals, knowing how to execute these fundamentals, and playing with enthusiasm. Football is played with both the head and the heart. The head learns how and when to perform a skill, while the heart provides the motivation to perform at the highest levels for every minute of every practice and during every second of every game. Another level of learning exists, however; another opportunity for the head to play an essential part in winning the game. The players should understand more than the fundamentals and how to execute them. They need to see the "big picture." They must understand how to win the multiple situations in which they may find themselves in the game.

Winning the Situation

The primary lessons described in this book start after the players have mastered the essential fundamentals, have learned when and where to apply the fundamentals, and are motivated to practice and play with enthusiasm. Important as they are, these three primary elements of success are not enough. Just because a team executes better doesn't necessarily mean that team will win the game. While better execution may help a team to win, it doesn't guarantee a win.

In some sports, such as track and field, the critical movements of the activity are well-defined. As such, track and field involves running, jumping, throwing, and other basic human movements. The fundamentals involved in these elements (and the degree of conditioning necessary to execute them at an appropriate level) remain constant in the competitive arena for each individual participant. In other sports, however, athletes face specialized situations to which they must react. In an individual sport such as tennis, how a particular situation is handled often determines who wins the match. With team sports, these situations take on an ever-increasing level of importance and managing them successfully becomes absolutely critical to winning.

In football, players need to be taught how to play what can be a very complex game. Compared to most sports, football has a wider variety of circumstances, more variables, and more players. Every play is a chess match that can result in a win or a loss. The coach must be an engineer who builds a team that performs efficiently in all facets of the game. It is the coach's job to develop a collective mentality in the team in order to help his athletes perform successfully in any game situation.

Practicing these situations is crucial for coaches at every competitive level. These impact areas should be planned for and practiced during the pre-season as well as during the season. As an example of how to teach the various situations that might arise in a game during training camp, a coach should employ a high-tempo, all-out hitting drill, followed by a very low-tempo, teaching situation. A coach should keep in mind that such a practice scenario is strictly a learning period.

All coaches should know on the day before practice what situations will be addressed in practice the next day. Every position coach should discuss what situations will be covered with his particular group before practice. Coaches should communicate with each other and with the players about how each situation should be handled. Players should understand how each situation will be handled so when they are on the field and a particular scenario arises, they will have a collective mentality on how to handle it. If nine players understand exactly how to handle the situation, but two are not part of that collective mentality, one of those two athletes might make the error that loses his team's advantage and possibly the game.

One of the major responsibilities of a head coach is to direct the development of the team's collective mentality. Of course, the coach must have a clear idea as to how the team should play. Just as visualization is important to the athlete and can have a positive impact on how the individual performs, the coach's "total" vision of how the team will win is essential to both the success of the season and the success in each game. The important point to remember is that the head coach, the assistants, and the team members must all be on the same page and have the same collective mentality if they are to play the game as a unified entity.

Planning for, and Winning, the Impact Areas of the Game

How to pick up the blitz? What to do in the two-minute situation? The coach should have a clear mental picture of how the team should respond in these situations. When he has that picture, he can build on his vision and develop his team's collective mentality. If he does not have a clear vision of how to respond to a particular situation, or if he has it but does not impart it to the players, then it is ridiculous for him to pound the table after the game and yell, "If we had only done this," or "If only that guy hadn't run out of bounds."

The team must be aware of and must practice the coach's vision. The coach shouldn't blame the team if the players haven't practiced a particular situation. Using a time-out to tell players what to do is not enough. If telling players what to do was sufficient to make them do it perfectly, they would not need to practice. Just give them a book of instructions and have them come back on game day.

Coaches who berate their teams for not doing things they have not practiced are no better than the second-guessers and armchair quarterbacks who know how to handle every situation after it has already happened. The effective coach must anticipate what might happen, and then must practice effectively to prepare for those possibilities. It is the coach's responsibility to have a comprehensive plan that allows the players enough time to learn how to handle the "what ifs" that often occur during the game.

The two-minute situation, for example, should be practiced with many possible scenarios. For example: From its own 38-yard line, a team runs a draw play on first down and makes 50 yards. Although such a gain is neither expected nor likely, the ball is now on the opponent's 12-yard line. This situation should be practiced: How should the offensive team practice that? How should the defense react to it? When a big play occurs in the two-minute situation, neither the offense nor the defense should be surprised.

Practicing in order to be fully prepared to handle the various circumstances that may occur during a football game presents a serious dilemma for coaches. Coaches cannot cover everything. Practices are not long enough to perfect every skill or address every situation. This fact is true whether the practice lasts an hour and a half or six hours. Is doing the carioca more valuable than a ball-protection drill? Is practicing 20 running plays or 25 pass patterns more important than practicing 10 plays and seven routes, and then working on ball stripping or punt blocking? Coaches should always keep in mind that a team will do well what it practices well.

The team's meeting and practice schedule should address the following aspects of play: sufficient red-zone offense so that the offense is confident it can score when it is in the scoring zone; taking a safety; taking a free kick after a fair catch when the opponent kicks a short punt (high school only); controlling the clock during the last minute or two of a half; calling time-outs during the last two minutes of a half; stripping the ball; long snaps under pressure; and big plays and when and where to use them.

Every coach should remember that time is the enemy. All practices and meetings should be used to work on what will help their team win. Coaches should have a theory of winning that is realistic, and then organize and conduct their practices to implement their vision.

A Typical High School or College Practice

A typical practice for many gridiron programs might include a warm-up, individual work, 15 to 30 minutes on the kicking game, group work, and then full-team offense and defense. However, the coach must also schedule time to practice those situations that may determine which team wins or loses the game. The coach can implement a number of steps to save valuable practice time. For example, if a high school has a freshman or junior varsity program, the team's basic offense should be learned at that level. If no lower-level program exists, a coach should simply reduce the number of offensive and defensive plays.

Above all, coaches must provide sufficient time to practice the situations that will make their teams better prepared to win the game. Among the key situations a team should practice, even if they are practiced only once per season, are the following:

• The passer has a pass blocked that he can catch. Should he catch it?

• The ball is snapped over the head of the punter.

- A partially blocked punt is on the kicker's side of the line of scrimmage.

- A partially blocked punt passes the line of scrimmage.

- The team with the ball is protecting a lead late in the game, and the ballcarrier is near the sidelines.

- The team with the ball is behind late in the game, and the ballcarrier is near the sidelines.

- The team with the ball is behind in the last two minutes and has just made a first down. Should the offense huddle?

- In high school, the opponent has punted from his end zone, and the receiving team has fair-caught the ball on the opponent's 20-yard line. What should the team do if it's behind by one or two points?

Frank Beamer, renowned head coach at Virginia Tech, has 50 such situations listed. He has his team work on all of them during early fall practices.

Fourth-and-goal on the two-yard line is another example of a situation that should be addressed in practice. A coach should have a vision of how to handle this situation against a particular opponent, and communicate with his team so they understand and can execute based on that vision. The team should know the fourth-and-two plays, practice them, and execute them in games. Coaches should always keep in mind that practicing the situations that can occur in a game is often more valuable than inserting more plays or more formations.

Former Dallas Cowboys and Miami Dolphins head coach Jimmy Johnson compiled statistics over the years showing that the following percentages work either for or against a team's ability to score from each zone on the field:

- Starting between the goal line and their own 25-yard line, the average team will score 7% to 12% of the time.

- From their own 25 to the 50-yard line, the average team scores 25% to 30% of the time.

- From the 50 to the opponent's 25-yard line, the average team scores 45% to 60% of the time.

- From the opponent's 25 to its goal line, the average is 80%.

The closer to the goal line the possession starts in each zone, the greater the odds of scoring. As evidenced by the statistics, most teams do not score on every possession. An opportunity for a long drive is often frustrated by an offensive penalty; a turnover; a big defensive play, such as a successful blitz; or a failure to convert on a third down. An unsuccessful drive usually ends with a punt or, if the team is close enough, a field goal attempt.

With regard to the impact of field position on a team's likelihood of scoring, Frank Beamer calculated probabilities that were lower than Johnson's findings. Starting inside a team's 20, he sees a 3% chance of scoring a touchdown. From their own 20 to the 40, about a 12% chance; from the 50, the likelihood of scoring is about 20%; from the opponent's 40, it increases to 33%; at the opponent's 20 the chances increase to 50%; and if a team gets the ball at the opponent's 10-yard line, its chances of scoring are about 50%.

Tilting the Odds

The odds can be tilted in a team's favor by paying particular attention to coaching the eight impact areas that often win or lose a game. The eight objectives that can increase the odds of winning include the following:

- Avoiding penalties

- Plus turnover ratio

- Big plays:

  - by the offense

  - denied by the defense

- Third-down conversions or defensive stops

- Blitz and blitz pick-up success

- Scoring in the scoring zones:

  - fringe

  - red zone

  - goal line

- Effective use of the clock:

  - end of half

  - end of game

- Kicking game (special teams)

Every impact area is extremely important. One game may be won or lost by the kicking game. Another may be won or lost because of failure to score in the scoring zone. Another outcome may be determined because a team won or lost the turnover or penalty battle. A team's level of performance in these impact areas can either help the team to win or cause it to lose.

A Philosophy of Coaching to Build A Team

With regard to coaching philosophy and coaching theory, it is important to note that the coach is the engineer who designs and assembles the team. The nuts and bolts of football are the fundamentals, assignments, execution, and the drills that help the players to learn the essentials. While this book focuses on how to improve a team's ability to handle situational football, it does not minimize the importance of fundamentals in any way. Fundamentals should be stressed at all times in mini-camps, training camp, and in meetings all year long. On the practice field, while working on the various situations that may occur, fundamentals should always be emphasized. Fundamentals can be taught during situational periods as well as during individual drills.

The coach should also teach the players how to compete. The desire and the ability to compete make up the personality and guts of a team. Every coach knows that motivation is an essential component of learning, having fun, and winning. Team motivation is more important in football than in any other sport. The theory of offense and defense, how to motivate, how much to emphasize toughness, enthusiasm, and team concept are all important factors.

After players have been taught the fundamentals of the sport, after they have been taught how to execute their assignments, and after they have developed the motivation to perform well and to win, the next step is to teach them how to play the game.

Football has been called a colliding chess match. It involves advancing or stopping the ball with hard contact and collisions. The key point is that it requires both a high level of coaching and playing intelligence.

The next factor that should be an integral part of a complete coaching philosophy is another primary focal point of this book. Players should be taught how to actually play the game of football. Just as the game of golf is theoretically quite simple, e.g., just hit the ball into the hole, the reality is quite different. A player seldom has the same shot twice. In one instance, he has an uphill lie 190 yards from the pin on the fourth hole at Spyglass Hill; the next time, he has a 190-yard shot from an uphill lie on the seventh fairway at St. Andrews. Although the distance to the pin is the same in both situations, these are two very different shots.

The same is true in football. A third-and-four on its own 40 when a team is ahead against one opponent is not the same as a third-and-four on its own 40 when the same team is leading a different opponent.

In golf, success is affected by how well the player executes the repeated fundamentals of the swing in various situations, combined with how well the individual manages the course. In football, success is affected by how well players execute their fundamentals and assignments, plus the effectiveness of the strategy and tactics a team employs during the game.

The fourth level in a sound football philosophy is to teach players how to play situational football. A coach must not only prepare the players to handle the situations that can arise in a game, but must also coach them to perform at a level that creates favorable situations for the team, such as increasing the takeaway ratio. In other words, the fourth level of a sound coaching philosophy is to teach the players how to play the game. In this regard, it is very important to practice the major types of situations that can occur in a game. No acceptable excuse exists for not practicing punting from the end zone, for not practicing how to take a safety, or for not covering in practice how to take a knee when ahead late in a half. A team cannot be successful if it does not work on minimizing penalties, recovering fumbles, or making the instant transition from defense to offense when a teammate intercepts a pass.

Football can be a very complicated game. Many players are involved (11 offensive and 11 defensive players at a time, plus a large number of substitutes and those players who participate on special teams). The ever-increasing number of rules, the ever-changing circumstances that occur during a game, and the many variables that exist within the context of the game are among the factors that must be handled successfully by coaches and players. All factors considered, the better the players can think and react to changing obstacles and opportunities, the more effective the team will be.

Coaches can't control every minute of the game. While the coach can call the play, the quarterback may have to audible in response to a defensive alignment. Therefore, the quarterback must be taught when and how to change a play. By the same token, the coach can call a particular defense, but the offensive set may require the defensive captain to change the defense. When and how to implement these changes are skills that must be taught.

The head coach is responsible for the broader issues that govern a team's approach, such as fundamentals, scheme, and motivation, but a team's week-to-week practices must take additional factors into account. A key point to remember is that winning is more than just fundamentals and execution. A team can be highly motivated and highly skilled, yet lose consistently if its players don't know how to deal effectively with the situations that can occur during the game.

Three of the most successful basketball coaches in the history of the game (Bobby Knight, Dean Smith, and John Wooden) made the practicing of special situations a critical part of every practice. In their approach, their primary focus was on preparing their teams for any situation, and spending less time and energy worrying about the opponent.

Although these three coaches certainly acknowledged the importance of fundamentals, a large part of their practices were devoted to creating and practicing situations the players might encounter in games. Then, when their players were faced with a similar situation in a game, they reacted very well because that particular situation had been practiced. The coach didn't need to call time-out to tell the players how to handle the situation because it had already been addressed in practice.

Attempting to coach players on how to handle a situation during a time-out is nearly impossible if that situation has never been addressed in practice. For example, a coach should not expect a sophomore quarterback to handle a critical situation successfully when the player is excited, tired, and the homecoming game is on the line, unless that situation has been practiced. It is not realistic for a coach to take a time-out and try to cram his players' heads with information and assignments that have not been practiced.

Coaches should work at least once early in the season on taking a safety. For example, the players could work on the following situation: The offense faces a fourth-and-five on their own six-yard line, and the team is ahead by three with a minute left in the game. The opponent will undoubtedly try to block a punt, so maximum protection will be needed. With maximum protection, coverage will be sacrificed. Without full coverage, the punt return will leave the opponent inside the 30, maybe even inside the 20-yard line. From this field position, the opponent will have a good chance to kick the tying field goal or to score a touchdown and win the game.

Taking a safety, on the other hand, means the team is still ahead by a point but can kick off from its own 20-yard line. As a rule, the kickoff will net about 40 yards, so the opponent should get the ball on about its own 40-yard line. In this instance, the opponent will have only one minute to cover 60 yards for a touchdown or gain 35 yards for a reasonable field goal attempt. Because the opponent will be in its two-minute offense, the defense should be confronted with fewer surprises.

For a coach at the high school level, another situation to practice at least once a season—better yet, on the day before the first game—is fair catching a short punt out of the end zone. If the receiving team is behind by one or two points late in the game or the half, the defense should rush the punt hard enough to hurry it while being careful not to rough the punter. If the punt returner makes the fair catch inside the 30 or 35-yard line, the ball should be in field goal range. In high school, after a fair catch, the rules allow the receiving team the chance to play a scrimmage down (first and ten), or take a free kick. The kickoff is also a free kick, but if the ball splits the uprights it does not count as a field goal. After a fair catch, however, a free kick can be taken to attempt a field goal. So, after a fair catch in this situation, the receiving team should elect to take a free kick.

The kickoff team should take the field, making sure only 11 players are on the field. The ball should be teed up in the center of the field. To avoid any possible penalty, only the kicker should move. This tactic should produce an easy three points.

But what if the team hadn't practiced this special situation, and the coach was trying to explain what to do by sending out the kickoff team after the fair catch? In summary, if the coach thinks successful management of this situation may enable his team to win the game, he needs to plan putting pressure on the punter, making the fair catch, and taking the free kick.

To further illustrate this point, consider this game situation: 14 seconds remain in the game, and the offense is down by six points. A touchdown and extra point are needed to win. Only two more plays can be completed in the time remaining. The coaches are all talking through their headsets about what to do, but the players who have to win it on the field are not a part of either the discussion or the conclusion. If a time-out remains, it can be used to get with the team and draw a play in the dirt. But wouldn't it be better to have practiced this situation? The players would be familiar with the options available, so instead of calling a time-out, the coach would simply call one or two of the plays that had already been practiced.

Teams need to be drilled on how to win games. Take advantage of the opportunities that arise during a game. Don't let the opponents win those crucial situations.

A two-minute situation to practice might include these characteristics: The offense completes a long pass to the opponent's 12-yard line. No time-outs remain, the clock is momentarily stopped to reset the chains, 10 seconds remain in the game, and a touchdown is needed to win. The coach doesn't want to lose a game because he couldn't get the play in on time, or because he hastily called a play that had little chance for success. Practice a designed play for a specific situation every week. Give it a code word for easy recall. Games can be won with preparation for this situation.

Successful basketball coaches use the clock for many of the situations being practiced. Consider the following scenario: The clock shows six minutes. The white team is ahead by 18 points. The red team must run the full-court press without fouling and must score quickly when it gets the ball. The white team comes down the floor and a forward takes a quick jumper from the foul line. Whether he makes it or misses it, the white team's coach stops the action and asks, "Jim, why would you take a shot like that when we're 18 points up and 25 seconds are left on the shot clock? Explain to me what you were thinking." In the white team's situation, spending seconds is more important than making points. This scenario represents an ideal teaching situation.

A coach should devote a great amount of practice time to situational work with his team. On the first practice day after a game, for instance, the schedule should include a short warm-up followed by 12 minutes of individual drills. The rest of the practice should be dedicated to situational work. Another practice could include six or eight minutes of individual work followed by situational instruction. Fundamentals should be the focus during training camp, but during the season, situational practices based on how to win the next game should take top priority.

Many pro football teams practice in pads only on Wednesdays and Thursdays. They work on fundamentals and execution, but within a situational context. The defense might practice ball stripping techniques, for example, against a specific ballcarrier or quarterback they will face that week.

It would be incorrect to think coaches at the professional level are not teaching fundamentals during situational drills. On a pass play, for example, the offensive line coach might say, "Joe, get your hands in a little tighter." The defensive line coach might observe, "You didn't need to spin on that one. It would have been better to stay with your bull rush." While they are drilling the situations that may come up in a game, the coaches are also reinforcing fundamentals.

Have a Vision of How You Want Your Team to Look

As head coach, you should have a vision of how you want your team to look. A defensive coordinator should have a vision of how he wants his defense to look. A linebacker coach should have a vision of how he wants his linebackers to play. A coach must know what he wants before he can prepare his team to execute during the situations that arise in a game.

For example, suppose the team's next opponent brings a lot of people on defense. The offensive line should spend considerable practice time during the week on picking up the blitz. If the line can't provide this protection effectively, the team's quarterback will spend much of the game on the ground.

A coach who organizes his practices efficiently doesn't necessarily have to give up time for situational work in order to focus on important fundamentals. Whether the areas where extra emphasis are needed involve blocking, tackling, proper positions, or other basics, the coach can incorporate the reinforcement of these fundamentals into situational instruction.

Some coaches have a session early in practice called "first things first." This approach can be used by either a head coach or a position coach, and it often takes place at the beginning of practice on Tuesday and Wednesday. The offensive linemen do bags, boards, and chutes every day. The defensive backs might work on open field tackling and playing the deep ball every day. The quarterbacks and wideouts might work on deep passes because they will need to throw deep on game day. The game evaluation should not show missed receivers on deep balls. All players are then drilled repeatedly on the skills necessary to execute in the upcoming game.

During individual work in practice, position coaches should focus on the areas they think are most important for the season or for the upcoming game. All coaches must see the big picture. For example, if the offensive line has been working on blitz pick-up for several weeks, but then the running game stops working, the problem may be a lack of focus on getting off the ball or not enough work on the bags, boards, and chutes. In another instance, if the safeties are missing open-field tackles, perhaps they worked so much on motion adjustments that they didn't have time for open-field tackling drills.

A coach must have a vision of what he wants his team to be. Every day of spring practice should include work on bags, boards, and chutes, as well as work on the essential offensive, defensive, and kicking fundamentals that are necessary to team building.

As the season goes on, the coach can reduce the time spent on some of these drills and still keep the players focused and sharp. The normal 12 minutes on bags, boards, and chutes every day should be enough to remind them of what they did all spring. The players simply have to practice perfectly a small percentage of what they already know. The "first things first" session, however, should keep its place as an important part of every successful practice.

The entire coaching staff needs to subscribe to the same philosophy and must be on the same page. Each coach should believe in teaching situational football while continuing to teach and review the fundamentals to ensure the effective execution of assignments. A collective mentality as a staff is a critical component of success. It is the coaches' job first to teach the individual groups, and then to teach the team as a whole.

Mike Singletary, college and professional Hall of Famer, has talked about the importance of making and sticking to communications. The following are a few of his observations that relate to the personal and staff level of involvement in the coaching philosophy described in this chapter.

- Have a vision of what you want to do.

- Write it down and refer to it daily.

- Follow through on the written vision.

- Without a commitment, it won't happen. This statement is true whether it's family or football, work or religion.

2

The Hidden Statistics

Although statistics don't lie, often they must be closely examined in order to get the complete picture. For example, the team that gains the most total yards in a football game usually wins. Each yard counts the same—yards gained by running, yards gained by passing, yards gained by punting, and yards gained from penalties. The example in Figure 2-1 presents a hypothetical, but common, set of game statistics.

Wildcats		Cougars
200	net yards rushing	100
20	passes attempted	10
10	passes completed	5
125	net yards passing	50
2	passes had intercepted	0
3	number of punts	6
90	yardage on punts	180
20	return yardage	30
3	fumbles lost	0
1	blocked punts	0
435	total yards	360

Figure 2-1

An initial glance at these statistics would suggest the Wildcats won because they had a 75-yard edge in total yards. However, the importance of one key statistic cannot overshadow others that may be just as important in a given game. Turnovers, big plays, red zone offense and defense, and hidden yardage are also critical. The Cougars intercepted two passes, recovered three fumbles, and blocked a punt; these statistics proved far more significant than the Wildcats' advantage in yards gained.

Each lost fumble typically costs a team 40 or more yards: The team didn't gain the punt yardage and the opportunity to gain more first downs is lost. Each interception of a short pass is worth 30 to 40 yards. Long passes intercepted are not as harmful, especially if they are 40 yards or more, because the yardage involved is similar to that of a punt. A blocked kick is often worth as much as 50 yards.

Because of the importance of turnovers, the 360 total yards shown for the Cougars was effectively much higher. It included at least 60 yards on the two interceptions, 120 yards on the three fumbles recovered, and 50 yards on the blocked kick.

Coaches who are focused on overall team performance look at the total picture, so they are more likely to work on techniques such as ball stripping on defense and ball protection techniques on offense. They work on fumble recovery techniques, effective punt blocking techniques, and correct loose ball pick-up skills for the non-blocking rushers. Coaches focused on the total picture are more likely to work on execution in the kicking game and forcing their opponents into mistakes.

To further illustrate these factors, consider the statistics from the following two real games involving teams A, B, and C, all real college teams of a few years ago. In the first game, Team A had 22 first downs; Team B had 12. Team A ran 87 plays for 502 yards in 36 minutes of possession, while Team B ran 51 plays for 247 yards in 23 minutes. Team A certainly won the joust. At the end of the game, however, the scoreboard showed Team A's 25 points and Team B's 27 points. How did Team A lose the game?

For starters, Team A had six penalties for 42 yards. Team B had only two penalties for 15 yards. Team A had five give-aways, while Team B had none. Much of Team A's great ball movement never got the team into the scoring zone because the offense turned the ball over. Team A had no big plays in the game. Team B had 126 more net yards on punts than Team A. Net yardage on kick returns was nearly even. Team A missed its only field goal attempt, while Team B was two for two. In the scoring zone, because of take-aways and a missed field goal, Team A got only two touchdowns in its three trips to the red zone. Team B had only one drive into the scoring zone, but they scored a touchdown. They recovered a fumble in the red zone and kicked a field goal, and they also scored on another give-away. Figure 2-2 shows the game statistics.

Team A featured two outstanding running backs; they ended their college careers as numbers two and three on the all-time list of ground gainers for that school. They were

	Team A	Team B
First downs	22	12
Plays/yards	87/502	51/247
Time of possession	36:51	23:09
Penalties/yards	6/42	2/15
Fumbles lost	5	0
Big plays	0	1
Kicking game		
Punts/average	3/49	7/39
Total yards punting	147	273
Returns	0	0
Field goals	0/1	2/2
Scoring zone/points	3/14	1/7
Scoring zone efficiency	67%	100%
Final score	25	27

Figure 2-2

largely responsible for the 500-plus yards of offense in that game. They were also responsible for the five take-aways.

Team A's coach made the decision to bench them for the next game because their fumbles caused Team A to lose. The next week they played Team C, an excellent squad that would finish the season 11-1. The replacement running back did not fumble, no give-aways occurred, and Team A was able to inflict the only loss of the season on Team C.

Team A had 13 first downs; Team C had 22. Team C had 437 yards of total offense to Team A's 135. Team C had the ball for 35 minutes, while Team A had it for only 24. But, Team A scored 13 points and Team C managed only six. How did it happen? Team A had four penalties for 30 yards, but Team C committed 14 infractions for 163 yards. Team A "outgained" Team C in penalties by 133 yards. Team A had only one give-away, while Team C had three. Team A had one big play, but Team C had none. Team A picked up about 90 yards in the punt differential, and Team C had 60 more yards on kick returns.

Team A ended up in good shape, in terms of total yardage because 163 of those yards were penalty yards. Team A got in the scoring zone once and scored. Team C was in the scoring zone six times, but managed only two field goals. They had the potential to score 42 points but scored only six. Figure 2-3 shows the game statistics.

	Team A	**Team C**
First downs	13	22
Plays/yards	58/175	79/437
Time of possession	24:33	35:27
Penalties/yards	4/30	14/163
Fumbles lost	1	3
Big plays	1	0
Kicking game		
Punts/avg	7/51	6/36
Total punt yards	357	216
Returns	1/75	1/18
Scoring zone/points	1/7	6/6
Scoring zone efficiency	100%	28%
Score	13	6

Figure 2-3

By adding the 175 yards from plays, 357 yards from punts, and 75 yards from the punt return, and then subtracting the 30 yards of penalties, Team A had 557 total yards. For Team C, 437 yards of total offense plus 216 yards on punts and 18 for the punt return, minus 163 yards in penalties, equals 508 total yards. The total yardage statistics for the two teams are close at this point, but Team A gets another 80 yards by virtue of its +2 turnover margin. This addition brings Team A's yardage total to 660, which represents a 150-yard advantage over Team C. Team A had one big play, while Team C had none, and Team A's efficiency in the scoring zone was superior to Team C's.

Despite what the statistics might suggest, the winning team played the best game of football in both of the examples presented in this chapter. The losing team in the second example, for instance, had 14 penalties and five turnovers, missed an easy field goal, and blew a coverage that resulted in a score for Team A. Team C also got into the scoring zone six times, but because of penalties and turnovers, scored only six points.

In general, for every 100 yards of statistical superiority, a team will generally gain at least one touchdown. So plan your season to be able to come out on top of the total statistical battle.

3

Avoid Penalties: The Internal Virus That Can Kill You

A virus can enter the body and make it sick; some viruses can even be fatal. Another kind of virus can enter a computer and cause it to malfunction or become inoperable. In football, the habit of incurring penalties can infect a team like a virus and cause it to be ineffective. Winning at football is difficult enough without the additional handicap of excessive penalties.

Coach Bobby Bowden of Florida State University believes that penalties are coaching mistakes. Many penalties can be eliminated with effective coaching. Avoiding penalties is a very important part of the mental game of football.

Can you imagine any coach signing a contract to play a game where the terms of the contract mandated that he must start six of his possessions with a first-and-15, or a first-and-25? His team would be at a great disadvantage. But, any coach who allows his team to commit fouls, which lead to penalties, is putting his team in much the same position. By failing to eliminate excessive penalties, the coach forces his team to dominate its opponents in many other categories just to remain competitive.

Every coach wants to avoid penalties, but how much do they work on it? North Carolina, under legendary coach Dean Smith, consistently committed fewer fouls than their opponents. Visiting team fans would chant "Carolina refs, Carolina refs," as if Carolina was getting preferential treatment from the officials. In reality, the players were coached not to foul. For example, they would never try to block a perimeter jump shot.

When running and jumping to block an outside shot, the defender's momentum frequently carries him into the shooter. North Carolina players were taught to jump straight up, hoping to bother the shooter, perhaps making him increase the arc of his shot. After all, depending on the shooter, the outside shot has less chance of going in than two free throws. Why increase the odds for the shooter while committing a foul in the process?

Fouls impact a football game just as they do a basketball game. If a basketball team gives up 15 more fouls than the other team, then they will have to perform much better in all other areas in order to win the game. In football, for example, a five-yard defensive penalty on first down makes it first-and-five, while a similar offensive infraction makes it first-and-15. It doesn't take a genius to figure out that first-and-five is better than first-and-15, so how do you practice for it?

Some years ago, a junior college game in Los Angeles pitted two fierce rivals. One team was stronger, but it lost because the middle linebacker was called for nine 15-yard roughness penalties. The linebacker had tremendous physical skills, but his presence allowed the opponent to get first downs via penalties. These penalties led directly to the opponent's win.

A more dramatic example occurred between two four-year colleges. With 30 seconds left in the game, the offense scored a touchdown to trail by a single point. They went for two and failed, but a yellow flag signaled an infraction: The defense had 12 men on the field. After a yard-and-a-half penalty, the offense went for two again. They made the two-point conversion and won the game.

Not all penalties affect the outcome of the game so dramatically in the final seconds, but any penalty at any time can ultimately determine the outcome of the game. For instance, a minor five-yard motion penalty on third down on the 40 might stop the scoring drive that would have produced the winning points for the team that incurred the penalty.

Often it is not only the penalty itself, but also the situation in which the penalty occurs that makes the penalty even more critical. An offside penalty when a teammate blocks a kick, or a block in the back that nullifies a long gain on a kick return, are common examples of the added significance of poorly-timed penalties. A holding penalty against the offense in the red zone may cost the team much more than 10 yards. It may mean the difference between a touchdown and a field goal, or it may take the offense out of field goal range altogether. In the same manner, an offensive penalty in the two-minute situation can cause an offense to lose its momentum, thereby reducing its chances of scoring. On the other hand, a defensive penalty in the last two minutes can be the impetus needed by the offense to drive for the winning score.

Practice to Avoid Penalties

The Oakland Raiders had a good season in 2002 and made it to the Super Bowl. In that championship game, however, the Raiders committed three defensive offside infractions that aided Tampa Bay drives. Three defensive offside penalties are inexcusable when a defender needs only to watch the ball as his signal to charge. Of course, the Buccaneers sacked Oakland quarterback Rich Gannon five times and returned three of his five interceptions for touchdowns, but those penalties eliminated any chance the Raiders had to turn the tide of the game. The next year the Raiders had a dismal season, one that prompted former coach Bill Callahan to say in December of 2003, "The Raiders are the dumbest team in football." He later revised his statement to say the players were not dumb, but they were playing dumb as a team.

How do you make your team play smarter? Some high school and youth teams bring in a parent or fan, or use a manager, to watch only for offside infractions when they do group work or play a scrimmage. This person doesn't have to be a trained official to see if a player lined up offside or jumped.

A running back can lean prematurely and be called for illegal motion, an unfortunate move that can be avoided if he is coached merely to bend his knees and touch the ground with his fingers. If the back stands tall in order to see the defense, the coach can teach him to have his weight either back on his heels or balanced. If the back can't get moving quickly enough from that position, then he should move another foot or two closer to the line of scrimmage.

For kick return blocking, the importance of blocking only in the chest of the cover man should be reinforced. If it isn't taught and practiced, eagerness on the part of a blocker may nullify a long return. There should always be a strong emphasis on reducing penalties. Whether at the youth, high school, or professional level, players must be responsible for all penalties except delay of game—coaches must take responsibility for that error.

A winning philosophy will bring success in any team sport. The principles are always the same: Increase the level of team performance, and win the big games. Stay focused on the game and don't give it to your opponents through stupid or illegal playing. Whether the approach to the game is wide open or conservative, these principles stay the same.

Teach Your Players the Important Rules

It is unfortunate, but true, that some players and coaches simply don't understand the rules. Sometimes they assume that a rule in the pro game applies to their level of football as well. For example, the professional rule that allows only one bump on a receiver—and it must be within five yards of the line of scrimmage—does not exist at the college or high school level. The pros put it in to increase scoring by passing. Some teams were so good at bump-and-run coverage that they were taking away much of the opposition's passing game. The owners eliminated that rule so receivers could run more freely. In fact, the use of hands on an offensive player was originally allowed to protect the defender from a blocker. The use of hands evolved into a pass defense technique as the passing game became more sophisticated and man-to-man defense became more common.

In another often-mistaken difference in the rules, a pro receiver must touch both feet inbounds in order to complete a catch. At the lower levels, only one foot inbounds is necessary for a successful reception.

Double forward passes, releasing players downfield on screens, a live ball on a bounced lateral pass, and releasing interior linemen downfield before a punt are just some of the situations in which the rules differ at the high school, college, and professional level. Even some officials don't always know the rules.

Most players know the rules about offside, for instance, but they don't often know the rules about the legal clipping zone. The American Football Coaches Association's Ethics Committee, in fact, has recommended against blocking below the waist in blind-side blocking in the legal clipping zone, but it is still legal. As another example, players often don't realize that a punted ball belongs to the return team unless touched by them. Return team members frequently gather around the punted ball when they should leave it alone. As a final rules example, the kickoff receiving team in a college game may not realize that a ball kicked into the end zone is live and may be recovered by the kicking team for a touchdown. In high school, however, the play is blown dead if the ball reaches the end zone on a kickoff.

With the complexity of the rules and their various interpretations, it is important for coaches to teach their players the rules for their level of competition, and then hold them responsible for playing according to those rules.

You Get What You Demand

Coaches get exactly what they demand. Players must be responsible for their decisions on the field. Coaches should advise, "If you're not sure, don't." "Don't take a shot if it might be a clip." "Don't get close to the punter unless you know you can touch the ball." "Play the whistle, even anticipate the whistle."

Players who are responsible will do the little things that win games. Failure to avoid penalties can cause a team to lose. If the best offensive lineman on the team gets two holding penalties or two illegal procedure penalties in a game, he hurts the team. Statistics denote that these penalties usually force the offense to punt. If a player repeatedly commits avoidable penalties, then the coach must inform him that his mistakes are causing the team to lose, and he cannot continue to play.

The coach must help players learn the right way to fulfill their responsibilities on the field. To help a player think about and eliminate those actions that hurt the team, the coach might make the player run the stadium steps, roll the length of the field, or perform some other punishment. But, what is the one thing a player values the most? He values playing time. Don't let him play until he learns to stop hurting the team.

In team meetings, a coach can single out those players who committed penalties and enforce consequences of his own. In this way, the team knows what is expected. Taking away playing time should be used early in a player's career and early in the season, to make the point both to the player and to the team.

If a corner makes a questionable play in practice, for example, the play should be addressed immediately. Perhaps he made a good break on the ball, but he must be taught to play the ball, not the receiver, because illegal contact will likely be called in the game.

Statistics reveal how often an offensive penalty stalls a drive, and how many defensive penalties allow drives to continue. They can show how many times a kicking game penalty greatly changed a team's field position. A clip on a kickoff return for a touchdown, for instance, usually brings the ball back inside the receiving team's 25-yard line. A team cannot suffer many 75-yard penalties in a game and expect to win.

Coach for penalty reduction on the field in practice. Catch the fouls, called or uncalled, on the game tapes, and correct them. Develop the collective mentality that penalties are stupid; penalties make you lose. Emphasizing this concept will increase your winning percentage.

Players must be coached to be even more alert about penalties near the goal lines. Penalties in these situations can result in touchdowns on either end of the field.

Using officials at practices is always beneficial if they are available. However, many high schools and colleges do not have that luxury. Coaches may have other resources available to them, however: Perhaps former players can be recruited to officiate the scrimmages. They could be given specific guidelines about what to look for and how to communicate the foul. A local officials' association might welcome the opportunity to send their rookies to scrimmages for additional experience. Position coaches may have the best vantage point for seeing illegal or questionable actions. In any case, coaches must be diligent in teaching their players proper techniques and how to avoid illegal play that might result in a penalty.

The ball moves up and down the field, whether the ballcarrier carries it or the referee carries it. The yards all count the same. A team might win the jousting contest, with their offense beating the opponent's defense, but still lose the game by not taking care of the business of winning. If the offense is moving backwards, something is wrong with the team and the teaching.

In order to help players understand the rules, officials are often available to talk to teams. The rules are so complicated that few players or coaches know every rule or how to apply it in every situation. But, the coach must devote substantial practice time covering the penalties that are most likely to occur, such as offside, clipping, unnecessary roughness, "in the grasp" situations, illegal procedure, offensive and defensive holding, and other common infractions.

Coaches must promote a mindset that avoids those penalties that could be called "dumb mistakes." In many ways, coaching is similar to parenting. If parents allow their children's rooms to be messy, they will be messy. If they allow loud music, they will hear loud music. If a head coach allows his team to incur excessive, avoidable penalties, those penalties will continue to occur. Whatever is tolerated will be repeated.

Coaches can add a variation to wind sprints to help reduce offside penalties: When the offensive players run sprints, they leave on a snap count. Defensive players go on movement of the ball. The coach in charge of the sprints should shout out different snap counts to try to draw players offside. The objective is to get the players to concentrate on sound on offense, and on movement on defense.

Regarding penalties, every team starts on a level playing field. Committing or eliminating penalties has nothing to do with the team's budget, the size of its linemen, or the speed of its backs. Every coach can work to reduce his team's penalties, and he doesn't have to sacrifice team aggressiveness to accomplish this goal. The coach should channel aggressiveness: It shouldn't start before the snap, and it shouldn't include a block in the back or a low downfield block. The coach can also emphasize, for example, that every tackle must be low enough to avoid the ballcarrier's facemask, or to play the ball, not the man, when defending a pass.

4

The Turnover Ratio

In order for a football team to score, it must move the ball toward the goal line. Runs, passes, kicks and penalties are plays that move the football. But, every time a team forces a turnover, it takes that ball movement away from the opponent and puts itself in the driver's seat. Whether a team recovers a fumble, intercepts a pass, or blocks a kick, it takes away the opponent's chance to move the ball and creates its own opportunity for a scoring drive.

If a team can protect the ball and prevent turnovers, it minimizes the opponent's chance to take control of the ball. Ball possession after a turnover often occurs in good field position. Current Dallas Cowboys coach Bill Parcells has noted that a team with a +2 turnover ratio generally wins the game.

The following actual professional game clearly illustrates the importance of turnovers on winning. Team A had a bad snap on their first punt of the game. Team B recovered inside the five-yard line and took an early 7-0 lead. Late in the game, the score was 13-6 with Team B on top. Team A had the ball at Team B's ten-yard line. The quarterback passed for what could have been a tying touchdown, but the pass was intercepted in the end zone. Team A ran a play that Team B had worked against in practice, so the defensive back was prepared for it. Not only did he intercept the pass, but the defender was also disciplined enough to stay in the end zone. The smart play allowed Team B to start at the 20-yard line.

Team B soon had to punt and Team A returned to Team B's 42-yard line with 2:30 to go. Team A went into its two-minute offense. The first play was a draw. Team B's right defensive end came around from behind and stripped the ball. A defensive back plucked the ball from the air and returned it 48 yards for a touchdown to expand Team B's lead to 20-6. The last two plays, executed by players who had been prepared for these situations in practice, were absolutely critical to Team B's win.

Team B's victory didn't rely on luck. The team had practiced red zone defense, including the exact pass play in which the interception occurred. They had also worked on ball disruption techniques. With 1:23 left in the game, Team B intercepted a pass that ended Team A's chances. One turnover caused by Team A's long snapper and three turnovers caused by other players were pivotal plays of the game. So, no matter how high the level of play, turnovers, or the prevention of turnovers, can cause a team to win or lose a game.

A five-year study of NFL games showed that teams with a +1 turnover ratio won 67% of their games. With a +2 ratio the winning percentage was 82%, and with a +3 advantage in turnovers the team won 91% of the time. One college coach also found that from the same position on the field, a team starting an offensive possession after forcing a turnover was more likely to score than if it began after receiving a punt or kickoff. The momentum the offense gains from the turnover, coupled with the letdown of the opponent, is an important intangible in increasing scoring potential.

In the turnover battle it is very important for the defensive team to put heavy pressure on the ball, while the offense must focus on protecting the ball. Luck is responsible for some turnovers, but most turnovers reflect how well the team has been prepared for the turnover battle. With a fumble, for example, perhaps the ballcarrier wasn't drilled on how to hold the ball. Maybe he was simply careless. On the defensive side, players should be taught how to strip the ball, and not to depend on a ballcarrier's carelessness.

A coach should never depend on fate. Luck is only a small part of success. Every coach should look at what he can do to increase his team's take-aways.

A starting point in developing a plan to cause more turnovers is to go beyond the offensive and defensive schemes, and to find ways to make players more productive in terms of giving the offense more possessions. An attitude about creating turnovers must be instilled in the defense. The defensive team should realize there is no one player more valuable to the defense than the player who creates take-aways.

A coach can take many steps to increase turnovers. One approach is to talk with other coaches about how to teach ball disruption techniques. Look for new drills that might increase teaching effectiveness. Look at the most likely situations where the odds would be favorable for disrupting the ball. Look at disrupting the ball from ballcarriers;

at how to effectively rush the quarterback to increase knockdowns; at how to cause fumbles when the rusher gets to the passer before he has thrown the ball; and how to disrupt passes through knockdowns or interceptions. Look at assigning a member of the coaching staff to lead development of a disruptive style of defensive activity. Some coaches prohibit defensive linemen from knocking down passes in practice because they want to let the offense complete their passes. In reality, passes do get knocked down during games. Some quarterbacks never see defenders with their hands up in practice, so they may have insufficient experience with knockdowns and strip sacks. Coaches who want to focus on creating more turnovers should re-examine their practice procedures and develop more game-like situations for the defense. Remember, a direct relationship exists between number of takeaways and number of wins.

Because their players were taught and drilled in practice, John Wooden, Bobby Knight, and Dean Smith always coached teams that played great defense by putting pressure on the ball. Players were taught to see their man and be aware of the ball. If a defender was close enough to the dribbler and the ball had just left his hand on the way to the floor, the player was taught to drive his hand under his opponent's and pick up the ball as it comes off the floor. The resulting steal—a turnover—is worth about a point per possession, according to basketball statistics.

The strategy of putting pressure on the ball works equally well in football. Before each game, study the opponent and determine which tactics are most likely to produce take-aways. Show videos of the opponent to illustrate how take-aways can be achieved against a particular team. Devote some practice time every day to ball disruption techniques.

Look at disrupting the ball from specific ballcarriers. Does the runner always carry the ball in his right arm? If so, there is a better chance of stripping the ball when the runner moves to his left. Look at how to rush a particular quarterback to increase knockdowns, and how to cause fumbles when you get to the passer before he has thrown the ball. Determine how to disrupt passes up the field through knockdowns or interceptions. Do not limit the practice to your game plan, pattern reads, or fundamentals. Consider how to disrupt your opponent's prime players. Spend planning time on how to strip or sack the quarterback, how to get an interception or a knockdown, and how to cause a fumble.

Keeping Statistics

Keep offensive and defensive statistics in order to measure the effectiveness of your turnover efforts. Keep statistics on interceptions and strips, and passes knocked down by linemen. Knockdowns count against the offensive linemen or the quarterback. Interceptions count against the receivers. These statistics become part of each player's grade sheet for the game, for the season, and for his career.

Maintain a category called altered throws. These plays often go unnoticed until the game tape is graded. On a play where the ball was too high or too far behind the receiver, the quarterback may have been forced to throw it to that spot because the passing lane had been altered by the defense. A defensive linemen may have had his arm up in a position that altered the aim of the passer. In this case, the lineman gets credit for the altered throw.

Expect your defensive linemen to force at least three altered throws per game. This goal is significant because it reduces the quarterback's completion percentage, which hampers the opponent's ability to move the ball.

Some altered throws are forced at more critical times than others. If the quarterback is forced to throw an incomplete pass on third-and-four, the disruption forces a punt. If the altered throw occurs in the red zone, it decreases the offense's chances of scoring. If the throw is altered on fourth down, it eliminates an offensive threat. Take special note of altered throws and knockdowns in third down situations.

Ball Awareness Leads to Ball Disruption

Ball disruption starts with an awareness of the ball's location. This includes awareness of where and how the quarterback holds the ball, and how each ballcarrier holds the ball. Study game tapes and determine which players are most likely to turn the ball over. For example, if a quarterback makes his drop with his arms wide, the blind side rusher can see his elbow and might be able to strip the ball from behind. Another quarterback may tend to throw high if rushers get their hands up. If a ballcarrier holds his arms loose or takes the ball away from his body when he makes a cut, he is vulnerable to fumbling. The coach should point these tendencies out to his players and practice ball-stripping techniques. (Figure 4-1)

Figure 4-1

Defensive players should practice getting at least one arm up on a pass rush. Sometimes a jump can be used to get extra height to block a pass. Jumping should not be used against a Doug Flutie-type quarterback, however. Scrambling quarterbacks feint passes to get defensive linemen in the air. Treat each quarterback differently, exploiting weaknesses as you discover them, but do not employ an overly aggressive scheme against a quarterback with sound fundamentals.

Consider this baseball-coaching scenario: Statistics show the opposing team likes to steal a lot. Does this mean every player steals equally well? Do one or two players get the majority of their steals? Is number 33 more likely to steal second base against a right-hander? Does that right-hander have a peculiarity that would encourage the steal, such as a bigger wind up? Does he forget to check the base runner once he starts his windup? Is number 27 more likely to steal third against a lefty? In other words, who steals and when do they steal? Armed with this information, the team is better prepared to prevent this opponent from stealing bases. Without this analysis, however, a lot of effort is largely wasted.

Use video analysis intelligently to determine the "who, what, and when" of important behavior by your opponents. Look for more than down and distance tendencies or formation tendencies. Look for more than formation and individual mismatches. Look for linemen who tend to jump on long counts or short motion plays. Is the quarterback too slow on his release? Which receivers can't handle bump and run coverage? Which ballcarrier carries the ball loosely? During the game, remind players about the tendencies you've discovered and how they can capitalize on them to get a take-away.

Stripping a Ballcarrier

During each week's scouting report to the team, indicate who handles the ball most often for the opponent and point out the most likely candidates for take-aways. In addition, report on how each ballcarrier carries the ball. Does he carry it in the right or left hand? Does he switch it to his outside arm?

If the opponents' best ballcarrier has fumbled only once in 400 carries, he is not a good candidate for a fumble. Shift your focus to another player on the opposing team. Always focus take-away efforts on individual players. The quarterback is usually the most vulnerable player when he is carrying the ball.

Whenever possible, try to simulate in practice which hand the opponents' primary ballcarrier uses to secure the ball. During drills, the ball can be placed in the proper arm to get the desired look. If the running back always carries the ball in his right arm and he is running to his left, work on stripping the ball. This increases the defense's awareness of potential opportunities for take-aways.

In practicing against the running game in a dummy scrimmage, instruct the defense not to tackle the ballcarrier, but to attempt to strip the ball. With all the swiping and grabbing, the ballcarriers get irritated at their teammates, but they like it when the defense gets a take-away in a game. As the defense practices ball-stripping, the running backs get practice at protecting the ball.

Ballcarrier Takeaway Drills

The "strip from behind" drill is often used in training camp. Have one player follow the ballcarrier. Don't be concerned early in the season with how the ball is carried, but as the season goes on, have the ballcarriers mimic the opposing running backs in the next game. A defensive player should see or sense the ball's location. He can't strip a ball if he doesn't know where it is.

Of course, a defender never wants to get into a situation in which he is trailing a ballcarrier. Individual defenders should find themselves in this position only once or twice in a game. Even so, the "trail and strip" drill must still be practiced. Perfect the techniques in training camp, then run this drill with every position at least once a week during the season. Start the drill on a yard line with the ballcarrier carrying the ball in either hand, with his elbow in or out. He runs down the line at about three-quarter speed with a defender trailing him by about a yard. The defender must first find the ball, then he should see if the ballcarrier's elbow is in or out to determine which technique he will use. First, the defender secures the tackle by grabbing the shoulder pads or wrapping his arms around the ballcarrier's waist (Figure 4-2).

Figure 4-2

If the elbow is in, he reaches around to pull the ball out. (The rake) (Figure 4-3) If the elbow is out, he reaches underneath to punch the ball out. (The punch) (Figures 4-4)

Figure 4-3

Figure 4-4

If the ball comes out, the defender chases the ball to recover it. If the ballcarrier has the ball in his right arm, it is best to take a swipe with the right arm and rip the ball downward. The left hand could be used instead to punch the ball upward. The left arm can also be used to attack the inside of the ballcarrier's elbow, while the right hand pulls at the ball.

As a defender approaches to tackle a ballcarrier who is carrying the ball on the near side, the tackler should put his head on the ball or try to rip it as he makes the tackle. If the ball is in the away arm, but the defender should simply secure the tackle.

The second defender on the tackle should attempt to strip the ball if the ballcarrier is secured. An effective technique calls for the second tackler to hit with his shoulder, but rather than wrapping up, he lifts the elbow of the arm carrying the ball with his outside hand, then punches the ball past the elbow with the inside arm. (Figure 4-5)

Figure 4-5

The free–arm swipe is an effective technique when a blocked defender cannot separate from the block but has one arm free. He should swipe at a ball being carried in the arm nearest him, and try to cause a fumble. In a free-arm swipe drill, the blocker doesn't try to level the defender; he just straightens his arms and locks him out. The ballcarrier must carry the ball in the arm closest to the blocker. The tackler can't separate from the block, so he uses his free arm to take a swipe at the ball.

Many of these skills can be practiced during the off-season. Drills could be performed while resting between sets in the weight room, for example, or they could become additional stations in the circuit.

In the defensive gauntlet drill (Figure 4-6), defenders do not stop the runner's movement, but they hit the ball and push and pull the ballcarrier's elbow. If they are on the ball's far side, they take swipes at the ball. The ballcarrier runs the gauntlet from each direction while keeping the ball in the same arm. The defenders alternate between attacking the ball on the near and far side.

Quarterback Strip Drills with the Quarterback in the Pocket

Because he can throw interceptions and he can fumble, the quarterback is usually the number one offender in terms of losing the ball. During drills, do not allow defenders to tackle your quarterbacks, but instruct them to strip the ball.

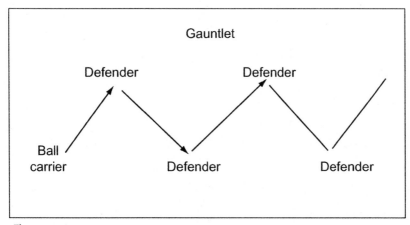

Figure 4-6

In dummy scrimmages, tell defenders to try to disrupt the pass and knock it down. The quarterback should gain experience with disrupted passing lanes so he can learn to make adjustments. The quarterback learns that he is the player most likely to fumble, so he must give extra thought to protecting the ball on his drops and set-ups. It is a common misconception that interceptions are a quarterback's most important give-away, but fumbles are usually more significant: A fumble recovered seven yards behind the line of scrimmage has a much greater impact than an interception with no 30 yards downfield.

Quarterbacks often carry the ball in positions a coach would never allow from a running back. If a quarterback holds his passing arm wide when he is set up, the defense may have a chance to steal the ball. If he scrambles only to his right, the defense should be aware of that to prepare for the sack. Coaches should focus the defense on more than getting the sack, however. Defenders should be focused on getting the ball.

If the defense is facing a loose-armed, right-handed passer, coach the right defensive end to secure the sack with his left arm, but to use his right arm to club the ball. Simulate this situation and practice the appropriate move all week long. Remind the right defensive end to look for this opportunity during the game.

The defender must first secure the tackle by grabbing the top of the quarterback's shoulder pads with the left arm. The next move is a punch through the gap between the quarterback's arm and his body. If the rusher can see the forearm, he can get to the ball. Using the same principle for quarterbacks that was described for ballcarriers, the defender punches up if the quarterback's elbow is out, or reaches around if the passer keeps his elbow in.

All players who may be involved in the pass rush should be schooled in these stripping techniques and opportunities. If a defensive back will be involved in a blitz, he should also learn the quarterback's tendencies and should practice the same ball-stripping techniques.

Interceptions

The dropping of a sure interception is a common sight in football games. The drop sometimes occurs even when the defender has a clear field in front of him. To minimize errors related to interceptions, they should be drilled every day in practice with anyone who might catch a pass, whether he is on offense or defense.

Depending on the level of coaching, emphasis can be placed on those coaching points that are appropriate to the group being drilled. Organize several lines for three to six players in a group, with a passer stationed 20 yards away from the first player in each group. Have the first man in line run fast toward the passer. The speed of running into the ball will make it more difficult to catch. (Figure 4-7)

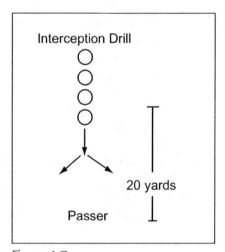

Figure 4-7

Coaching points include:

- For the first part of the drill, the passer throws the ball high. The receiver should be taught to overlap his thumbs and index fingers as he catches the ball. The speed of the ball will tend to separate the hands, and the receiver should catch it on the near half of the ball. If he tries to catch the middle of the ball, it usually will go through his hands. (Figure 4-8)

Figure 4-8

- Instruct catchers never to allow the ball to go through their hands. If the ball goes through a defender's hands, the receiver is likely to catch it for a touchdown. Instead, if the catcher does not catch the ball, he should make sure the ball drops in front of him. In fact, by blocking the ball and keeping it in front of him, a defender has a second chance to make the catch.

- Once the catcher masters catching a high ball with his thumbs in, start throwing low to make him catch balls with his thumbs out.

- For the next progression, have the passers look right or left and throw in that direction. The catcher must now move in the direction of the passer's eyes (or jaw) to catch the ball.

- For the last part of the drill, have the catcher dive to catch the ball, while making sure his elbows and forearms are under the ball so it will be caught before it hits the ground. (Figure 4-9)

Figure 4-9. Diving catch

During this drill, the interceptor should yell "Pass!" when the passer holds the ball high, "Ball!" when the ball is released, "Got it!" when the ball is coming toward him, and "Oskie!", "Bingo!", or "Fire!" when the ball has been caught and tucked away.

When the interceptors have mastered running straight at the passer, split the line to put interceptors 15 yards outside the passer so the ball can be thrown to them at an angle. (Figure 4-10)

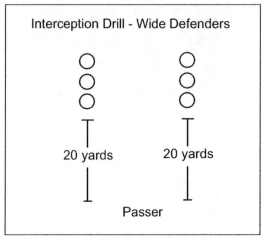

4-10. Interception drill

Pass Disruption Drills

Players should be coached to always try to disrupt the ball in the air. Front-line rushers should defend the passing lanes and attempt to disrupt the quarterback in order to get sacks and strips. If a rusher is on the same side to which the passer is looking and is "Velcroed" on the blocker, then he has been stopped. He won't get a sack, but he can still help to disrupt the pass. The defensive lineman is not merely trying to penetrate the passing lane, but also trying to knock the ball down.

Trying to knock the ball down is even more important against quick passes, because the rush will probably not get to the quarterback. When a defender is rushing a passer and the ball is thrown, the defender should reach up with the arm nearest the direction in which the quarterback is looking and attempt to knock the ball down. Even if the rusher doesn't knock the ball down, he can still alter the quarterback's throw. He might make the quarterback throw a bit higher, or throw around him, or make the quarterback alter his arm motion. Any factor that forces the quarterback to alter his throw reduces the chances of a completion and increases the chances for an interception.

When rushing a sprint-out quarterback, the rusher should run at the quarterback and raise his arms toward the direction of the throw when the quarterback raises his passing arm. The rusher wants to knock the ball down, but even if he fails to touch it he will still force the quarterback to alter his pass.

A similar tactic is used in basketball: If a defender is directly in front of a right-handed shooter who jumps, the defender jumps and raises his left hand. If the defender is overplaying the shooter to his right, he would raise his right arm if it is closest to the ball. It certainly doesn't make sense to raise an arm that doesn't have a chance to touch the ball.

"Passes knocked down" is a category that should be graded, and stats should be posted every week so everyone knows who has performed well in this area. Coaches cannot expect passes to be knocked down if that expectation is not communicated to the team. This aspect of pass defense must be emphasized and drilled in practice.

If a rusher is on the backside of the quarterback, he should continue his rush because raising his arms will have no effect. In fact, the passer may be forced to turn back because of a strong rush or effective coverage, so the rusher should be balanced and ready to make the tackle.

Coaches should also drill linebackers on these hands-up techniques: With the inside backers on a middle blitz, put up two bags as offensive linemen. Have a passer drop and throw to a catcher downfield. Move the catcher right, middle and left. As the passer sets to throw, the linebacker's near hand should come up to hit the ball. When an outside linebacker blitzes, place the catcher wide because the throw is to the outside. As the passing arm goes up, the linebacker's hand should go up, but the defender must continue his rush because the passer could pull the ball down.

Practice the Situations That Happen in a Game

Every coach wants his defense to knock passes down, but players must practice the proper techniques in order to meet the coach's expectations. A pass will be knocked down by accident on occasion, but knock-downs will happen much more frequently if practiced. A coach may have to reduce the time used in another drill in order to emphasize this goal. A coach must decide how he wants his team to look, and then practice the things that will make his vision a reality.

Prepare the defensive linemen by having them practice against specific plays you expect to see in the game. If the opposing quarterback throws a lot of three-step drop passes, there should be opportunities for knock-downs. If the quarterback has a low delivery, the defense should focus on knocking down passes.

For example, imagine a third-and-four situation against a "sticks" offense, a team that often goes for the first down just a yard or two beyond the first down marker. The quarterback is likely to throw the ball at the sticks with a short drop and quick throw pattern. The chances for a sack are minimal, but the ball will be thrown low. The pass rusher understands the situation and knows he will have a good opportunity to knock the pass down. He is prepared to take advantage of the opportunity because he has studied the opponent and practiced the techniques. The defense needs to know the opponent's tendencies in terms of down and distance and position on the field. This tilts the odds in the defense's favor.

If the offensive team sends out four wide receivers, the defense should yell, "Dime, Dime!" The coach will signal the appropriate defense, but he will not have time to shout, "Fourth-and-three, watch the short drop, quick throws, watch the out cuts and slants, draw, and short middle. Keep your hands up and knock the ball down." If the defense doesn't already know that information, they couldn't remember it anyway. But, if this situation has been practiced during the season, and especially during the week, they know what to expect and what to do because of the collective mentality that has been developed for this situation.

When the quarterback takes a short drop, such as on third-and-four or in the red zone, he is likely to throw quick slants, quick outs, or a fade in the red zone. The defense is unlikely to get a sack. But, the quarterback will be throwing in lanes where the primary rushers have a good shot at knocking the pass down. Therefore, the defense must have a collective awareness involving all players who should be looking for the quick drop and the possible knock-down. The odds are higher for knocking down passes in the red zone than on any other spot on the field.

In the red zone, altered throws or knock-downs can be point differential plays. An altered throw or knock-down might deny a touchdown and force the opponent to settle for a field goal. In such a case, the knock-down is essentially a four-point play.

Players should know that if they're in the defensive red zone, the quarterback probably will throw either a fade or an out cut. Players need to practice this situation in order to be prepared.

Defending the Receiver

Coaches should drill linebackers on stripping the ball from upfield receivers. As the backer follows the receiver, throw the ball out in front of the receiver. The linebacker reaches for the receiver's arm with his downfield arm (the arm closer to the passer). The backer should try not to hit the arm with his upfield arm, (the one closer to the receiver), as he may bump him with his shoulder and be called for pass interference. Emphasize the importance of avoiding interference penalties during this drill.

For a pass to be complete, the ball must end up in the receiver's hands. If the defender looks back for the ball, it might pass him and find its way into the receiver's hands. But, if he watches the receiver's hands and stays close, he can get to the arm when the hands come up. By practicing this technique, good defenders will learn to sense when the ball is about to arrive.

The defender must make a critical judgment when he doesn't know whether to play the ball or the man. In general, he should go for the hands or the ball when the man is close. If the receiver is farther away, the defender should secure the tackle and forget the ball. If the receiver is close, the defender can play his hands. If the receiver is very close and his hands go out, the defender can look for an interception. As part of the practice warm-up, a coach might have two players jog together, and then throw the ball to the receiver and have the defender try to knock the ball up or down.

Some coaches teach their defensive backs a technique for stripping the receiver of the incoming ball. With the defender on the receiver's hip, as the receiver's hands go up to catch the ball, the defender grabs the receiver's far shoulder or shoulder pads with the nearest hand. He simultaneously reaches with his far arm and knocks down the nearest of the receiver's arms. (Figure 4-11) By the time the defender reacts to the receiver's hands coming up, the ball will have hit his hands. The defender is actually playing the ball.

Figure 4-11

Some defensive back coaches teach a similar technique, but instruct defenders to wait until they see the flash of the ball across the receiver's face before attacking him. Other coaches teach defenders to look for the ball and the pick as the receiver's arms come up. Some coaches tell the defender to watch the eyes of the receiver, because the eyes of most receivers will widen and focus as the ball approaches. Seeing this cue gives the defender an even earlier warning of the approach of the ball.

While defending against a hook pattern with the receiver in front, the defender should employ an up-to-down or down-to-up strip. The defender must get his arms inside the receiver's arms and rip them outward, taking both of the receiver's hands away from the ball. The bump of the defender's body must occur at the same time, or just a millisecond after, the ball touches the receiver. Well-timed contact gives the strip has a better chance of success. (Figures 4-12, 4-13, and 4-14)

Figure 4-12. Up to down strip

Figure 4-13. Up to down pass strip

Figure 4-14. Down to up strip

Recovering Fumbles

To properly recover a fumble, a player must dive beside the ball and wrap himself around it. Teams that are turnover-conscious start practicing fumble recoveries during the very first week of practice. Proper techniques should also be practiced during the week, and they can even be included in pre-game warm-ups.

While some coaches instruct their players merely to fall on any loose ball (a simple solution to a sometimes complicated situation), another option often exists. If he is pursuing a blocked kick, the player should pick up the ball and try to score. In other situations, a player might have a clear field, such as on an errant pitch, and he should attempt to score rather than just recovering the ball. For loose-ball situations that can lead to a score, have players practice scooping up the ball instead of falling on it. The player should get at least one hand under the ball, between the ball and the grass, and lift it. The most natural way to retrieve a ball on the ground is to just reach down and pick it up from the top, but that method is much less secure than the scoop. With the scoop, even if the player doesn't pick the ball up, he will still be rolling the ball toward the goal line and will have another shot at picking it up as he runs after it. Every kick-blocking team should devote significant time to this drill.

Ball Protection and Eliminating Fumbles

On the offensive side of the line of scrimmage, the importance of ball protection must be stressed and techniques for protecting the ball must be taught. A back who fumbles isn't worth much. A 100-yard rusher who loses two fumbles a game actually has a net yardage of about 20 yards, since every fumble lost is equivalent to at least one punt of 40 yards. If the running back carried the ball 20 times in a game, his effective average was not five yards per carry, but only one. Ball protection is essential.

A coach who wants to win will not play a ballcarrier who fumbles. He will, instead, play the non-fumbler who may not get as many yards but won't cause the team to lose.

The ballcarrier must keep hand and elbow pressure on the ball and protect it in traffic when he is being tackled. Some rushers like to keep the ball in one arm but bring it across the body when in traffic. (Figure 4-15) Others prefer to cover it with two hands when they are in traffic or when they are being tackled. Either technique is acceptable as long as the ballcarrier doesn't fumble. If a ballcarrier is prone to fumbling, teach him a secure way to carry the ball.

Figure 4-15

Emphasize how to apply the proper pressure points on the ball. If he can't hold on to the ball, let him watch the game from the bench. When a player fumbles in a game or during practice, some coaches make him carry the ball correctly for an entire day. Legendary coach John Heisman always began his first practice with the warning, "Gentlemen, this is a football. It is better to never have been born than to drop it."

Consider the real statistics on three recent NFL teams, shown in Figure 4-16. None of these teams was highly productive on offense, but they were able to minimize their own turnovers while capitalizing on those of their opponents. Their cumulative record was 37-11. Not bad for unproductive offenses!

	League rank in total offense	League rank in turnover ratio per game	Win/loss record
Team 1	26	2nd	12-4
Team 2	20	1st	13-3
Team 3 (1990 Giants)	17	1st	12-4 (won Super Bowl)

Figure 4-16

Drills To Prevent Fumbling

During part of the warm-up, instruct all ball handlers to carry footballs with them as they perform forward or shoulder rolls. Emphasize holding the ball tightly during the roll. A coach who uses the "dive and drive" drill to teach explosiveness should also make every ball carrier carry a football during this drill. Teach them to cover it with two hands as they hit the ground. In any running drills (high steps or bounding, for example), ballcarriers and receivers should carry a ball. They need to concentrate on the pressure points of hand and elbow as they run and hit the ground.

A coach should determine which techniques he wants to use for ball protection. When the back is in traffic or is being tackled, have him either put both arms around the ball, or bring it across his chest to make it more difficult to strip. The quarterback carries the ball either in two hands as he sprints out, or he carries it in one hand where it is easy to strip. The ballcarrier either carries the ball in his outside arm or he holds it with the same arm on all plays.

Some coaches teach players to carry the ball in only one arm, since shifting the ball often leads to fumbles. However, other coaches teach players to shift the ball away from potential tacklers. Each method has advantages and drawbacks. Emphasize ball protection in every drill in which a ballcarrier can handle the football, and make ballcarriers conscious of ball protection at all times.

Practice What You Want In a Game

One college team set a goal of causing three turnovers per day for each of their 15 pre-season practice days. Accomplishing this goal meant they would have forced 45 turnovers during that time. Setting goals is an important first step, but goals are reached only when work is directed toward achieving them. In the case of the college team's goal of three turnovers per day over fifteen practice days, the coaches made a board listing every practice from one to 15. They told the players they would put the name of any player who caused a turnover on the board for everyone to see. Most football players respond to challenges, and they like to do well in front of their peers. On the first day, the defense forced nine turnovers in drills and scrimmages. The name of each player who caused a turnover was listed on the board. The coaches broke down the practice video and cut out the turnover plays, but they didn't show this footage to the team.

The defense caused eight more turnovers on the second day of practice. More names went up on the board, and that day's turnovers were added to the turnover tape. The tape was set to music and shown to the team. As expected, the tape livened up the team meeting. As a result, every player wanted to get on the turnover tape. By the end of the 15 days, the defense had caused 72 turnovers. Another benefit was the fact that the offense was working harder than ever to protect the ball. Both lessons carried over into the season.

Use Practice Time to Teach What Will Win for You

Make all drills relate to game situations. Warm up by performing the same tasks that players do in the game. The following questions will help prioritize practice:

• What is essential to practice?

• What is very important?

• What is important?

• What would be good to know?

• What has very little importance?

• What is unimportant?

Start eliminating items from the bottom up, while making certain that practice includes what is essential and what is very important. Practice what will win, and remember that time is the enemy.

5

Big Plays

Some research indicates that big plays are far more important than time of possession in determining the outcome of a game. Big plays can be made by the offense, the defense, or the kicking teams. Sometimes big plays just happen, but more often they result from planning and practice.

Big Plays by the Offense

Most coaches want their offenses to make big plays, so these game-changing plays shouldn't happen only by chance. Coaches should look for opportunities by watching the opponent's game video. After noting the possibilities for big plays against the next opponent, the coach should work with the players during practice to teach them how to take advantage of the big plays. At the first offensive staff meeting of the week, the head coach should ask the other coaches if they have seen opportunities for big plays. bean opportunity might be in the form of a particular match-up, or a defensive adjustment to motion by the offense, or a pass pattern that seems to cause trouble for the opponent. An opportunity could also exist because of a defensive technique that can be exploited. Look for opportunities for big plays, practice them, and then call them.

In order to create big plays, the coaching staff needs to be look for possible openings on opponents' game videos. Some coaches believe it takes 13 men to defend effectively against an offense. Therefore, at least two openings should exist in every defensive alignment. One opening can often be found, for example, in the throwback area. On other occasions, the wide countering or reverse area may be exposed. Opportunities can be found most often in the area of pass defense, especially in pass defense zones. To take advantage of these particular openings, try to exploit certain coverages with different formations or motion. Try to get a receiver open with a simple read for your quarterback and receivers.

Position coaches drill their players on specific stances, reads, and techniques from the first day of practice. These techniques do not change during the game. Even if a key player is injured, his substitute will use the same techniques. Offensive players can gain an advantage on many if the defender tips off his intention. Coaches should teach players what to expect if they notice an extreme weight-forward stance, a defensive drop such as a bump-and-run or a press, or other telltale alignments.

By studying defenders closely, offensive players can almost feel as if they're in the huddle with them. If the corner always uses an outside alignment when he is playing zone, for instance, then he's unlikely ever to change. Smart offensive players will be ready to take advantage of this corner's alignment habit, because whatever the corner does from that setup will be wrong.

The following real game situation occurred because the offensive coaches had studied the opponent's game video and were able to exploit a weakness. In studying the game tapes of the opponent's defense, coaches noted the following opening: From a particular offensive formation on a running situation, with play-action to the strong side, sneaking the split end deep against the two-deep secondary gave the receiver an excellent chance to get open for a long completion. The opponent's corner was ineffective at jamming the split end, and the weak safety always moved toward the play-action. The best field position from which to run this play was the offensive right hash mark, because it gave the split end the most room to run a slim post.

The offense didn't see an opportunity to call the play in the first half. However, the opponent took the second half kickoff and eventually drove to the three-yard line, where they were stopped on the right hash mark on fourth down. The offensive play-caller had to overcome some resistance to calling this play from the three-yard line, but he prevailed and the play was called. Just as planned, the weak side safety drifted toward the middle, and the corner failed to jam the split end as he ran a slim post. The quarterback threw the ball on target for a 97-yard touchdown. If the ball had been on the 50, then the play would have resulted in a 50-yard touchdown. If the ball had been in the parking lot, then the play would have produced perhaps a 195-yard touchdown. The play was there for that situation!

The key factor in the previous situation was that everything was in place for the big play. The coaches accurately predicted the opponent's reactions. The play was practiced and confidence was developed in its potential for success. If the coach had been reluctant to call the play because of the field position, that 97-yard score would never have occurred.

Big plays are even more important when teams are evenly matched. If one team is vastly superior, then they should dominate their opponent. Most games, and big games in particular, don't pit mismatched teams against each other. Big plays can win those close games. Against a strong defense, few offenses will produce many 14-play, 80-yard drives. The right situation may arise only once in a game, so teams must be prepared to take advantage of it.

Match-ups are a very important part of the offensive game plan. A coach's primary offensive concern should be in finding match-ups that will help his team win. Formation match-ups may offer opportunities, but more often the openings will exist in individual match-ups. Examples of individual match-up advantages include getting the fastest receiver on the defense's slowest corner, or isolating a running back on the slowest linebacker.

Team match-up opportunities may not be as abundant, but taking advantage of them can be equally effective. As an example, when facing the Bears' 46 defense, the Raiders inserted three different blocking schemes in an attempt to control the defensive rush. When the Raiders employed a single scheme, the 46 defense overpowered the offensive line. However, with man, zone, and slide protections giving the offensive line opportunities to double-team the primary rushers, the Raiders' passing game became much more successful.

In some cases, a key match-up doesn't become evident until the game is under way. Some years ago the Chiefs began a game against Oakland with an unexpected five- or six-man rush that included two or three linebackers. Raiders coach Tom Flores noted that the Chiefs' defenders were playing man-to-man coverage on every play. Flores countered by placing a receiver in the slot on the split end side. He put the slot receiver in motion, leaving the split end (Cliff Branch) one-on-one with an entire field in which to work. Branch ran a corner fake, which turned the defender, and then he broke to the post and was wide open for the touchdown. After the touchdown, the Chiefs reverted to their traditional defense—the defense the Raiders had practiced against all week.

Big plays are much more likely to succeed if they are practiced in expected situations. Coaches who want their teams to be ready for big-play opportunities must leave enough time to practice those plays that can produce easy touchdowns.

Big Plays Must be Denied by the Defense

Big plays by the offense can change a game dramatically, but a few big plays by the defense can be equally significant. Big defensive plays can offset much of the opponent's advantage. An offense's ability to gain yardage does not guarantee a win;

the team must be able to move the ball across the goal line. Whether a team scores at the end of a 15-play drive or on a single big play, the results are the same. If the opponent has big-play capabilities, coaches must determine who is most likely to be involved and when those big plays are most likely to occur.

Study the opponent and identify which plays or players can cause your team to lose. Decide how to match up against their best rusher and their best receiver. Develop a plan to stop both the "who" and the "when"—the individual and the situation in which he will be used.

Most coaches have concluded a post-game analysis by saying, "We really played well. Except for those three big plays, it was our game." Those three plays could have been a 50-yard pass, a 19-yard pass, and a 19-yard run in a tough situation. Whether the plays resulted in three touchdowns or three critical first downs, they made the difference in the game. The defense didn't stop the big plays that won the game for the opponents.

A winning defense must stop both big plays and long drives. While its own penalties, missed assignments, or a turnover may stop a drive, a team can't count on its opponent to commit errors. The defense should be prepared to stop the opponent's offense by disrupting its drive with tactics such as a blitz, and by taking away its big-play potential.

Good coaches try to determine how the opponent sets up big plays. Some offenses try to create a formation or individual mismatch. Coaches should plan to put extra help on the opponent's big playmaker. Against a big-play receiver, for example, covering him man-to-man while the other defenders play zone can be effective. An inside-outside scheme against the receiver is another possibility. In another scenario, if the opposing offense is trying to get the ball to its best running back through screens and delays, the defensive response might be to let him catch the pass under the zone coverage. Another approach is to put a spy on the back to stop that five-yard pass and prevent the back from gaining 50 more yards.

Coaches should look for formation or down-and-distance tip-offs in order to be ready for big play attempts. Is the offense more likely to pass from a split-back set? Do their big plays usually come on first down, in a particular set with motion, outside their own 35? The more a coach knows about his opponents' tendencies, the better his ability to tip the odds in his team's favor. By discussing opponents' tendencies with the players, and by practicing against the situations, a collective mentality is developed that increases the odds of winning the big-play situations.

With proper preparation and execution, big plays can often be predicted and stopped. Why, then, would an intelligent team allow its opponent to do what it does best? Teams should strive to make an opponent's offense execute "left-handed" by forcing them to deviate from the game plan.

Even in a high school context, where it may not be feasible to put together specialized coverages, effective measures can be used to prevent big plays. The first step is to make sure players know what to expect. A coach might instruct the defense to play a corner bump-and-run on a talented wideout, but still play a full zone cover. He might tell his corner, "When they get inside our 50, you can be sure they're going deep to number 88. Be aware of it and don't let him get behind you, ever. If I call a three-deep coverage when they have a first-and-ten on our 42, understand why I am doing it. In five of their last six games, they have hit this kid deep in a first-and-ten situation on the offensive side of the 50."

Perhaps the upcoming opponent has a play that has worked very well for them, a play that will require extra practice time for the defense if they expect to stop it. The play could be a cross-buck, a reverse, or a screen. In the heat of battle, defensive players sometimes forget to do what they have practiced. The coach must either take a time-out, or talk to the players between series, to remind them that they have prepared for the situation. Getting a player to execute properly in a game is much easier when he has practiced and prepared during the week.

6

Third Downs

Third downs are similar to big plays because of the effect they can have on a game's outcome. A positive or negative third down result for the offense either continues or negates the progress made in the drive. A coach should not have to call a time-out to call a quarterback sneak on a third-and-one during a critical drive. It is important to practice third down situations because they are always critical for both the offense and the defense. Third down situations are impact areas for which the coach must plan and practice.

In some ways, third down situations are games unto themselves. They are the essential battles that frequently determine the outcome of games. An offense can continue a drive if it gets a first down, while a defense can stop an opponent's drive by denying a first down. Winning the third down situations can help a team to overcome other negative factors. Of course, it is desirable to make yards on first and second down; yardage gained on these plays make third downs easier to convert. Regardless of the yardage needed, however, third down is the pressure down. On either side of the ball, a team must win only one of the three downs. The team must win the third down situations.

The coach must always have a good third down plan. He should know what he wants to do, and the team should practice it. If sufficient practice time on third down situations means practice time for an extensive offensive plan must be reduced, then perhaps the offensive playbook itself should be trimmed. Once again, coaches must remember to practice what will help a team win.

First down play-action passes often work well, and these plays are usually practiced, but a third down play-action pass should also be practiced. In a third-and-four situation, for example, the opponent will probably be in a tight bump-and-run rather than a soft three-deep, so the tight coverage will offer receivers an opportunity to get to the sticks.

Some coaches practice only third down situations in scrimmages because they recognize the importance of winning the critical third-and-one, third-and-five, or third-and-15. If a coach doesn't script his scrimmages, he should at least strongly consider using the third down scrimmage idea.

Scripting Practice

Coaches should script the offensive practice versus expected defenses in each situation. In the same manner, coaches should script the defensive practice versus the opponent's offensive tendencies in each situation. Develop the collective mentality in your team regarding what to expect and when to expect it. Compare this year's play calls to those of earlier years against the same head coach or offensive coordinator. As a general rule, coaches don't change their thinking patterns greatly from year to year. If a coach's philosophy seems to have changed, determine whether it was due to a real change in thinking or a change in available personnel.

Both the third down scrimmage and scripting approaches are effective tools for coaching key situations, but more focused methods should also be used. Third down situations simulated in practice can be made more game-specific by practicing in red zone, goal line and two-minute scenarios. It may be productive to dedicate an entire practice day each week to nothing but third down situations.

The emphasis on the first day of practice during the season should be on run and play-action situations. Some third down work should be included, as well as defensive coverage repetitions against some of the upcoming opponent's pass patterns. On the second day of practice, most of the third down plays should be set up and practiced. First, second, and third down situations should be scripted on the third day. When planning the script, be sure to include enough third-and-four, third-and-six, third-and-long, and third-and-two plays. Encourage the team to think collectively and understand what the opponent is likely to do. Try to determine the opponent's theories of offense and defense, its game plan, and probable play calls.

A coach may not be able to accomplish everything at the high school or college level that can be achieved at the pro level, because professional coaches have access to their players for the entire week, every week of the season. The demands of meetings, practices, and walk-throughs would be impossible for a student to meet. However, coaches at all levels must prioritize available practice time; preparing his players to perform in third down situations must take a high priority.

The Must-Throw Situation

How can a team throw when it must throw? If the quarterback is too small to pass from the pocket, he should roll out or sprint out to give him a better chance to complete the pass. If the quarterback doesn't pass the ball effectively, then have him pitch the ball to a back who can throw. Nowhere in the rules does it state that all passes must be thrown by the quarterback.

When a coach starts his practice planning, he should focus immediately on what will be needed to win during the season. His practice plan, therefore, should feature those plays and techniques that will help the team win. For example, the quarterback must have the confidence that he can make the reads on a critical passing play, and the receivers should be certain of their roles. Coaches must plan and prepare for that crucial play, instead of reaching into the grab bag in search of the perfect solution. Put a third down plan in place, now!

"Win the game" plays should also be planned for and practiced on a regular basis. With five seconds left, behind by six points, with the ball on the two-, five-, or 12-yard line, the offense should know the play and how to execute it. They should be familiar with the situations in which the play would be called. The offense should also be able to execute this play on any down, from any number of formations.

The offense would commit a critical error, for example, if it tried but failed to stop the clock with five seconds remaining in the game. Other situations to plan for could include third-and-nine with three minutes to go, with the team either leading or trailing. The coach needs to have a plan that has been practiced for each of these situations.

It is a good idea to have a play that should work against any cover scheme: man, blitz, or zone. One such play is a shotgun, trips left, double slant with the inside man slanting out. If this is your offense's "gotta have it" play, then it should be a part of the team's theory of winning. It should be part of the week-to-week strategic plans.

The following points summarize the importance of third down situations:

• A third down situation determines who will have the ball on the next first-and-ten; most teams find it easier to score with the ball than without it.

• Third down success or failure either magnifies or negates the impact of preceding plays in the drive.

• Many third down possibilities exist, and each has its own best solution.

- Since third down situations are so critical, other offensive and defensive elements should be reduced in order to concentrate on third down offense and defense.

- Be excited about the challenge of the third down situation, and convey this enthusiasm to the team.

- Remember that you win with repetitions, not tricks.

A high school team doesn't need eight plays for every situation. But, the team should have one or two plays for each basic "gotta have it" scenario: third-and-two, third-and-four, third-and-eight, third-and-13. The following are examples of third down situations that should be scripted and practiced:

- 1 to 2 yards

- 3 yards

- 4 to 5 yards

- 6 to 9 yards

- 10 or more yards

7

The Blitz

The blitz is a dynamic member of the "impact family." In the same manner as a great actor, the blitz can play many roles and can change characters quickly. The blitz can be a leading actor who plays a main role, or it can be a bit player who appears only occasionally. The blitz can be a stable character whose appearances are expected in certain situations, or it can show up when least expected. The blitz can appear in a normal costume, such as a middle backer stunt, or in a more exotic disguise, such as a safety or corner blitz. In any character and at any time, the blitz can have a dramatic impact on the outcome of a drive and the game. Because of the blitz's importance, both the blitz and blitz pick-up should have more practice time dedicated to them than the coach would normally devote to plays that occurs so infrequently.

Some coaches do not consider blitz situations to be important because either they don't blitz much, or they don't see much blitzing from their opponents. These coaches don't feel the need to work on blitzing on defense, or to practice blitz pick-up on offense. Failure to prepare for and to practice blitzing and blitz pick-up will cause a team to lose at some point.

Effective blitzing and effective blitz pick-up don't happen by luck. As with other successful plays and techniques, they must be practiced. When these plays are properly executed, they can cause a team to win. When they are not performed properly, they will cause a team to lose. A single loss that occurred because the offense didn't work enough on blitz pick-up will probably make the coach wish the team had spent less time on carioca drills. Perhaps he will regret not working more on formation and motion adjustments for his blitz scheme and coverage.

No intelligent person makes an investment without analyzing the potential risks and rewards. Likewise, a football coach shouldn't call a play in which his team hasn't invested significant practice time.

Situations will arise in which a team needs to blitz, and other instances will force a team to pick up the blitz. These occasions will occur most frequently at critical points in games, and how the team responds will be a key factor in whether it wins or loses those games. Practice time for other aspects of the game may have to be sacrificed in order to focus on blitzes and blitz pick-ups. A coach's priorities are direct reflections of his coaching theory.

Attention must also be paid to telling the defense how to react if they are in a blitz, expecting a pass or an inside run, and the opponent runs a sweep instead. Some coaches teach the blitzers to abort the blitz and get in their pursuit lanes. Most coaches, however, teach the blitzers to continue through the gap, and then to adjust. The offense creates enough variables; the defense shouldn't complicate the situation. Some coaches tell the blitzers to continue the stunt if the offense runs a certain play, to pull back if the offense runs something else, and to trail if the offense chooses a third option. Such instructions are too complicated for the defense to consider during a play. The best approach is to proceed with the blitz, no matter which play the offense runs.

Planning the Blitz

Effective blitzing against a specific opponent requires significant planning. First, a coach should determine which blitzes have been successful against this opponent in the past. If they have had trouble with a strong-side two-backer blitz two weeks in a row, plan to test them with the same blitz. Perhaps the opponent failed to work on that blitz package again this week. Maybe they don't have a workable blitz pick-up package. Armed with this information, consider other types of blitzes that could be used against the opponent. If your strong safety isn't needed in coverage, he can be a part of the blitz package. Depending on the opponent's tendencies, a corner blitz might also be effective.

It is also important to know the opponent's plan versus the blitz. First, determine whether the opponent's receivers watch the near-side linebacker for a blitz. With this blitz pick-up approach, when a receiver sees a blitz, he yells, "Hot!" and releases into the linebacker's zone. Another offensive response to a blitz is to hold in the backs, or to release them quickly into "hot" patterns.

In blitz situations, does the opponent's offense go to maximum protection and throw? If so, which pass patterns do they run? Are they likely to throw slants, or is a run a possibility? The scouting report might reveal whether the likely runs will be quick pitches, sweeps, or draw traps. Does the quarterback scramble? In which direction is he most likely to run? Use this knowledge in your blitz scheme.

It is also important to plan how the defense should respond to non-dropback actions such as the waggle, bootleg, sprintout, or rollout. Assign players to contain the expected movement so the blitz can be successful.

A major key to blitz success is how well it is disguised. Blitzers should be great actors. Good blitzers also have keen instincts. Natural blitzers exist at every level from high school to the pros. On the other hand, physical limitations may eliminate some players from being good blitzers. In most cases, for example, the strong safety weighing 145 pounds will be blocked by the 185-pound running back. The 220-pound linebacker represents a better chance to execute a successful blitz.

In recent years, teams have had success blitzing with nickel or dime substitutions from the slot cover man. As in the previous example, however, if the linebacker on that side is the better blitzer, he should stay in the game. It makes no sense to use a peashooter when you want a .357 Magnum on a blitz. A coach may be forced to change his blitzing strategy to take advantage of his best blitz personnel.

Effective blitzing often results in quarterback sacks, fumbles, and wins. If a coach wants his team to win, he must make sure his team is able both to blitz and to handle the blitz.

Playing Man Coverage Behind the Blitz

Man coverage, and especially bump-and-run, should be considered when blitzing in a pass situation. Whether or not the free safety blitzes, the defense must still cover five receivers. A defender assigned to a running back should engage him and occupy his block if the back stays in the backfield. If the back releases into a pass pattern, then the defender should play him man-to-man. (Figure 7-1)

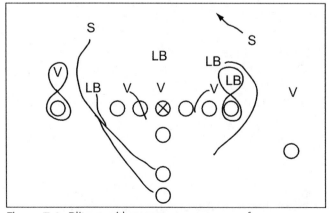

Figure 7-1. Blitzes with man-to-man or man-free coverage

Playing Zone Behind the Blitz

In addition to playing man-to-man when blitzing, many teams also use zone cover behind the blitz. This scheme usually involves either a four-under or a three-under, two-deep zone. The defensive coordinator will often slide the zones to protect the most likely target area, and he may also drop off a lineman to cover a zone or to spy for a draw or screen. Playing a zone behind the blitz allows for much better run recognition and frees more defenders to react to the ball and to potential receivers. (Figure 7-2)

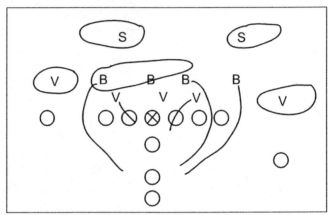

Figure 7-2. Zone blitzers

Blitz Pick-Up

A few years ago a major motel chain promoted its inns with the slogan, "No bad surprises." This slogan also applies to an offensive unit's alertness to the blitz. Nothing can blow apart an offensive play as quickly as an effective blitz. "Bad surprises" range from a yardage loss, to an interception or fumble, to an injury to a ballcarrier or quarterback from a blind-side hit. Every "bad surprise" takes it toll, so the offense must be prepared to neutralize any blitz.

The entire offensive unit, including staff and players, should be on a constant red alert for a blitz. At any level of football, the quarterback should be instructed and drilled to be prepared for the blitz and to know how to react. The quarterback must be aware of the clues a defense might offer to indicate a blitz, including tight bump-and-run coverage, linebackers or safeties who have moved up, or an important substitution. A single offensive player who is asleep at the switch can cause a disaster. Blitz pick-up is another area for which the coach must develop a collective mentality. When an offense has developed a high level of confidence in its ability to pick up and exploit the blitz, it plays with a confident attitude. Sufficient practice time is the only way to develop that kind of confidence in the offensive team.

The coach should spot the opponent's blitz situations and alignments as he studies game tapes. He can then instruct the offense and lead them in practice to prepare for the blitzers. A good blitz analysis might indicate, for example, that the upcoming opponent blitzes more than the other teams he has coached against so far this season. Perhaps the opposing defense is more likely to blitz on its side of the 50. The coach might observe that the backers usually sneak up a bit and that the cover people come up from eight to about six yards. The coach is now prepared to give his quarterback a good picture of what to expect, and when. The tight end and slot back should look for the same tipoffs and should be alert to make the hot call when the near backer moves. A play that could have been a sack can turn into a 10-yard completion because the offense was prepared and had practiced against the blitz.

The offense's preparation should include pre-snap blitz looks, but it should still be prepared for a well-disguised blitz after the snap. Decide on a key for the running backs to use on whether to block or release. Decide on whether to zone block or use a man-to-man protection scheme, and determine who will block the probable blitzers in a blitz situation. Decide whether or not to use hot calls, and determine which players should make the calls.

The offensive game plan might require adjustment if the coach expects the next opponent to blitz. Inside plays like traps or wedges might work. The wedge works well when defenders are crossing and not charging low. Outside runs, such as toss sweeps and options, are often effective. Use zone blocking to run away from inside penetration by linebackers while controlling the outside charge of linemen.

An effective method for zone blocking on wide running plays is to block the down defensive linemen with either the lineman in front of him or the one outside. If the defender is in a gap, the offensive lineman to his inside should reach-block him so the outside blocker can release for second-level blocking on a backer.

Zone Blocking Techniques

The first blocker to make contact with a defensive lineman should step first with his outside foot to prevent an outside charge, and then move his inside foot into a better blocking position (even crossing over). He blocks with his inside shoulder or hands (inside hand on breastbone, outside hand under outside armpit of defender). When the inside blocker makes contact, the first blocker stays with the block for two steps, and then releases outside to move to the next level and contact any backer coming at him.

The first blocker does not need to take the outside position if the defender's position is inside shade or inside gap. However, he should still make shoulder or hand contact and stay with the block until the inside man contacts the defender. The first blocker may then release to the next level.

The second blocker to make contact is the inside blocker. His split should have been reduced to make this move easier. He steps with his near foot and tries to get his head in front of the defender. He drives with his shoulder or gets leverage by using his hands (inside hand to the midline of the body on or below the breast bone, outside hand under the armpit or to the outside of the defender). To avoid a holding call, the blocker must keep his hands inside the blocker's shoulders. (Figure 7-3)

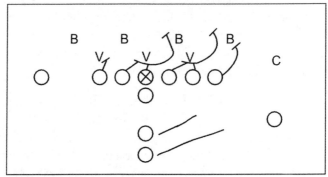

Figure 7-3. Zone blocking for outside run plays

Pass Protection Versus the Blitz

Depending on the level of play and the sophistication of the passing offense, an offense can pass-protect with either man-to-man blocking, zone blocking, or both. With man blocking, the linemen responsible for blocking the backers may have to drop deeper if they see their man stunting in another direction. Assignments are easier to teach and to learn with man protection. If an opponent has an outstanding rusher, the offensive line can slide toward him and double-team him. (Figure 7-4)

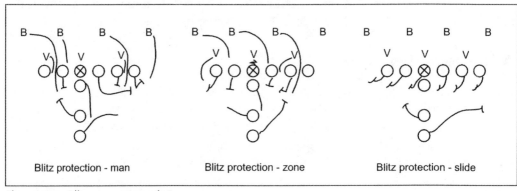

Figure 7-4. Blitz pass protection

Essentials for the Blitzing Defense

• Disguise is critical to the success of a blitz. The blitzer should not tip his hand with his alignment, facial expression, or body language.

• Attack the protection.

- Know how the opponent has picked up blitzes in the past.

- What blitzes have given the opponent problems in other games?

- Decide which defenders should be involved in the blitz. The choice of personnel may differ depending on the objective of the blitz, such as sacking the quarterback or stuffing a run.

Essentials for Blitz Pick-up

Avoid bad surprises by answering the following questions:

- How often does the opponent blitz?

- What are their tendencies?

- When will they be likely to blitz?

  - Do they give any tipoffs?

  - Do they show a bump-and-run or other man cover?

  - Do the backers sneak up?

  - Do their corners sneak up?

  - Do they substitute a certain player or players?

- What types of blitzes do they use?

  - Inside with inside backers or strong safety inside?

  - Perimeter with the corner, outside backer, or safety in a wide blitz? Do they use an outside stunt?

- Are they most likely to blitz from a zone or man defense?

- Can you get a "hot" read?

  - With which personnel are they most likely to blitz?

  - Who are their key blitzers? Are there any defenders who never blitz?

  - What abilities do their cover people have? If they blitz, where is your best chance of getting a completion?

8

Scoring Zones

Teams should practice scoring every day to maximize scoring potential. Effective ball movement, particularly in the scoring zones, generally determines who wins the game. Therefore, red zone attack and defense are extremely interesting to plan for and to practice. Coaches must concentrate their efforts so players can play with intelligence, intensity, and impact in the scoring zones.

A team may complete four 15-yard curls or drive the ball 60 yards, but unless these efforts show up on the scoreboard, the effort is just exercise. Statistics such as 200 yards of rushing offense or a 60-percent pass completion rate are commendable, but the records that last are the ones that appear in the win-loss column.

Practicing Scoring Will Increase Your Wins

Some very effective teams do most of their practice from the opponent's 40 to the goal line. If a play is effective in the fringe area, it can probably work just as well inside the 20 or near midfield.

The coach should reward an offense that works hard to get the ball into the red zone by making sure they have a good chance to score. Jousting between the twenties doesn't win the game; what happens inside each team's 20- or 30-yard line usually determines the outcome. Another way to increase the team's likelihood of success in the red zone is to practice goal line offense every day during spring practice. Use the best players, whether they play offense or defense, and put them on the goal line offensive team. If the starting linebacker is the best goal line fullback, that's where he should play. Help the players get excited about being able to score. Teach that sense of urgency! Be excited! Work harder! Get the score!

Some coaches argue against taking away the linebacker's primary responsibility in the previous example, but nothing is more important to a team than scoring touchdowns. Therefore, do not get into a goal line offense situation without the best personnel, the best preparation, and the most knowledge about how to score. A team might run only six plays, but in spring practice they should run them live every day.

Points alone determine the winner. Therefore, when the offense has a good opportunity to get points, they must take advantage. A team must have an effective scheme for scoring, and they must practice it. Every coach admires an offensive team that seems to get hungrier when it can see the goal line. Every team can have that hunger and the ability to feed it, but only through planning and practice.

Create Scoring Situations

To make his offense an effective scoring machine, the coach must have the team practice its best goal line plays in a number of situations. On one practice day, the offense runs only third-and-two plays for a situation in which the team is six points behind. The offense must score. On the next day the offense works on a fourth-and-five, "must score" situation. On another day the situation could be the last play of the game, from the opponent's 15 or 20, with the offense needing a touchdown to win.

On the defensive side of the ball, players should be learning and practicing against what offenses do on the goal line. A couple of extra stops in goal line situations by a well-prepared defense might result in two more wins. Games can be won by strong goal line play by either the goal line offense or the goal line defense.

Two analogies from other sports point to the importance of actually scoring points versus simply running plays. In golf, the object is to get the ball in the hole in as few strokes as possible. Top teaching professionals emphasize that the best way for the high-handicap golfer to lower his score is not to go to the driving range and slam away for distance, but rather to spend about 70 percent of his time practicing shots that will help him score from 100 yards in. The approach shots, the pitches and chips, and the putts are the shots that actually put the ball in the hole.

In basketball, imagine how ridiculous it would be for a team to spend two hours running fast breaks and set plays without ever attempting a shot. Such a practice strategy might result in a lot of open shots, but it wouldn't convert to points on the scoreboard.

Scoring is another impact area that must be planned for and practiced. If a coach wants his team to look like a scoring machine, then it must practice scoring.

The area of the field between the 30 and the 20 is called the *fringe* area. The area between the 20 and the goal line is the *red zone*. The red zone can be segmented even further into four sub-areas: the 20 to the 15, the 14 to the ten, the nine to the five, and from the four to the goal line. From about the five-yard line, or wherever the opponent starts its goal line defense, is the goal line section of the red zone. Figure 8-1 summarizes these zones.

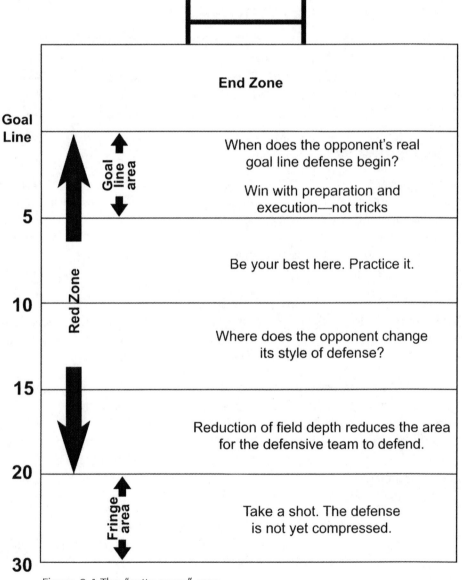

Figure 8-1.The "gotta score" area.

All three scoring zones provide opportunities for an offense to execute scoring plays. Develop a scoring plan with specific concepts and plays for each zone. Teams that work hard on their red zone games will develop not only competency in play execution but also greater motivation in their team. Competency and motivation breed confidence, and confidence in execution is far superior to mere creativity.

Confidence enables a team to play more effectively. The other impact areas that have been discussed become even more important as a team advances toward the goal line or is backed up deep in its own territory. The importance of avoiding a penalty, causing a fumble, thwarting a blitz, or converting on third or fourth down are all magnified in the scoring zone. Attention to these impact areas in every practice makes goal line offenses and defenses more productive. Like several streams flowing together to make a rushing river, hard work in each of these impact areas will combine to make a team far more effective where it counts the most.

The importance of penalty avoidance, particularly by the offense, cannot be overemphasized. A holding penalty on the ten against the offense costs the full 10 yards, whereas the defense is penalized only half the distance to the goal. A penalty stepped off from the thirty may put the kicker out of range and cost the team three points. A penalty incurred at the 10-yard line may cost the offense four points. Penalties in this area of the field are much more than annoyances; they can cause a team to lose a game.

Turnovers are equally damaging in the scoring zone. Even teams who haven't been effectively drilled on stripping the ball know they most focus on that tactic on this part of the field. Ball security becomes increasingly important for ballcarriers in the red zone. Quarterbacks must learn to expect more pressure in the red zone, and they should be more aware of protecting the ball. A strip-sack denies the offense of three to seven points. The defense must be prepared to cause a strip-sack; the offense must be prepared to prevent it.

The Fringe Zone

The fringe zone offers great opportunities to utilize the talents of the quarterback and receiver. The defense isn't so compressed that it can ignore the deep routes. The offense shouldn't be afraid to take a shot at the end zone from this position. Streaks, posts, and corners can be run in this zone. Once the offense gets to the 10-yard line, however, the compressed defense eliminates deep routes and can employ much tighter coverages. The offense will start to see eight- and nine-man fronts, and scoring a touchdown will become increasingly difficult. Therefore, if an opportunity exists to get a score from farther out, why not take a shot?

Red Zone Offense

The level of play in the red zone is more competitive than anywhere else on the field. Scoring or denying points here determines winners and losers. The coach must determine which offenses and defenses can be used in this zone, and he must place a high priority on practicing them. For the offense, plan how to score and practice it. For the defense, plan how to deny the score and practice it.

In general, defenses are more predictable in the scoring zone, particularly inside the 20. Try to determine the opponent's defensive tendencies in this zone: When do they blitz, how often do they blitz, and in what down and distance situations are they likely to blitz? Be prepared to exploit the blitz when it occurs. If the defense plays more man-under, use double-breaking patterns, hooks, and curls. If the linebackers play tighter, consider running wide.

Remember the "first things first" concept: In order to score from the fringe, the scoring plays must be practiced. Have the quarterback throw deep patterns and look for mismatches in formations or personnel. Field space is also critical; the offense may run out of space to throw certain patterns, and the defense will change to reflect that advantage. As the defense changes, the offense must keep looking for new advantages. Is coverage a man-to-man match-up zone in which a receiver might be able to shake free? Will a crossing pattern or boot action work? Would an option work, or a quick trap?

Many teams increase their defensive blitzing in their red zone, but other teams blitz very infrequently. Most defenses do not play any three-deep in the red zone. Let the quarterback know which plays will be called in the expected blitz situation and give him the opportunity to beat those blitzes. Teach the linemen and backs how to pick up goal line blitzes. Teach the offense the plays that will take advantage of the expected blitzes, and practice them often. Remember that there are always at least two openings in a defense, so find them.

Goal Line Offense

It is important for the offense to know when the defense actually changes into their goal line scheme. If they are in man-to-man, how do they contain the quarterback? Is the bootleg open? Will crossing patterns work? What about a run-pass option?

The coach must also know his own team. If the offense has an advantage in physical power, then the coach can reduce the number of formations and get into a jousting contest. If his team is not a big physical team, or if the opponents have the power advantage, the coach may choose to spread the offense to force the defense to spread as well. A coach must consider many possibilities. For example, will more be gained from the offense being bunched or spread? What is the best way to get our best players matched against their weakest players? Can a mismatch be created through motion? Creating a mismatch might involve putting a wide receiver into a setback position where he is likely to be covered by a slower backer, and then motioning him out and using crosses or picks to get him open.

The coach should look at the scouting report to find specific weaknesses. Be specific in how to exploit these weaknesses, and run plays that will work in this situation. Putting in a special play for that week's goal line attack may not be as wise as running the basic goal line offense. Instead, try running basic plays with simple wrinkles, such as a different set or with motion. Pick the tried and true plays based on personnel or formation matchups.

The coach should also try to determine whether the opponent plays zone rather than man coverage in the red zone. Do they change coverages? When are the opponents most likely to go into man coverage? Crossing patterns often work versus a man-to-man defense. For example, use a wing or inside slot set, hook the outside receiver, and then have the outside receiver come back under the coverage. This creates a screen much like those used in basketball.

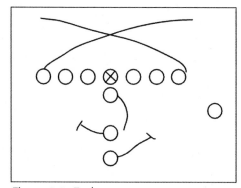

Figure 8-2. Ends cross

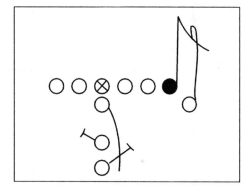

Figure 8-3. Hook and cross from slot set

With the crossing pattern, the pass must be delivered at the right instant to give the receiver the most clearance. Timing is critical for all goal line patterns, but it is especially important for crosses. (Figure 8-4)

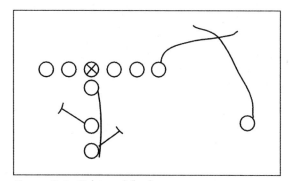

Figure 8-4. Tight end-flanker cross

If the coach is unable to determine whether the opponent will be in a man, zone, or blitz package, he should have adjustments receivers can make when they recognize the coverage. Many teams use receiver reads all over the field, so it is not necessary for receivers to learn them only for the red zone attack. A flood pattern with a hook, or one that breaks sharply away from the man coverage, may be a good starting play. When the flanker and flanker-side running back encounter man-to-man coverage, they can run away to free themselves. (Figure 8-5)

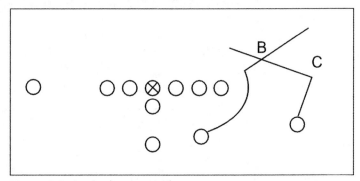

Figure 8-5. A win the game play

Another play to run is the wing-end cross, as described earlier, but with another receiver coming higher into the zone. This twist provides a crossing pattern versus man coverage and high-low receivers if the coverage turns out to be a zone. The passer has to look in only one area of the field. If no one is open, then the quarterback can throw the ball over the head of the deep man and out of the end zone. Prepare the quarterback for the "no chance" scenario when he is passing near the goal line, so he knows when to throw the ball away to avoid a sack. (Figure 8-6)

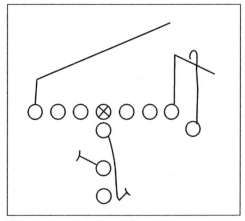

Figure 8-6. High-low with a cross

For running plays on the goal line, emphasize to the linemen that they should keep driving until their shoulders cross the goal line. The offense should have a running back who isn't afraid to go up and over. The up-and-over can be practiced by putting a stack of blocking dummies or a high jump pit in the defensive area, and then letting the back practice taking deep handoffs and jumping up and over as he protects the ball.

Because of the hard charge of the defensive linemen, a quick trap can also be effective. If the trap is used, caution the backs to be ready to jump over the legs of the linemen. The jump legs trap" has been a successful play for many teams in the goal line situation. (Figure 8-7)

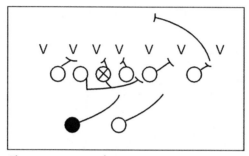

Figure 8-7. Jump leg trap

Goal Line Offense in the Closing Seconds

Part of the goal line offense plan should include how to handle the offense in the final seconds, when a touchdown is needed to win. The plan can be broken down as shown

Situtation	Clock running	Clock stopped
First inside the 10		
First inside the 5		
First inside the 2		
Second inside the 10		
Second inside the 6		
Second inside the 2		
Third inside the 10		
Third inside the 5		
Third inside the 2		
Must score down on last play of the game, or fourth down plan:		
Inside the 10		
Inside the 5		
Inside the 2		

Figure 8-8

in Figure 8-8, which presents a number of situations that the coach should plan for. He should have a formation or play that fits into several of the slots. The number of time-outs remaining would also factor into the decision to run or throw. An option team can probably run the option in many, if not all, of these situations. A run-pass option would also fit into several of these slots. A passing team would probably use the fade as a preferred play. The following examples illustrate some possible play calls in specific situations:

- With the clock stopped and the ball inside the five on second down, run the triple option.

- With the clock running and the ball at the three, use the run-pass option with the pass as a last resort. The pass will either score or stop the clock.

- Use a run-pass option or a pass from outside the five, but run basic bread-and-butter plays inside the five.

- With the clock running, 10 seconds remaining, third-and-six, run a fade or crossing pattern to score a touchdown or stop the clock for one more play.

Red Zone Defense

Particular attention should be given to red zone defense when scouting the opponent. For purposes of defense, divide the red zone into three areas in terms of scouting: the 20 to the 15, the 14 to the ten, and the nine to the four. Try to determine whether the opponent's offense runs seam patterns from farther out in the red zone. What about crossing patterns as they get closer? Do they run hard crosses or picks?

When scouting the opponent, take note of whether the team tries to win the game with plays or with players. Do they substitute a player only to run the ball? Do they like to throw to the tight end? Do they keep most of the same people in but change their play selection? Do they run bootlegs or crossing patterns? Do they change formations? Most coaches are somewhat predictable in the approaches they use for specific situations. Knowing what's coming is half the battle when preparing to face the weapons in your opponent's arsenal.

The coach should try to determine the opponent's strategy for getting the ball into the end zone. Most teams run more crossing patterns to confuse assignments or to pick defenders with screens. Slants are also used closer to the goal line. The coach should also determine the type of running plays the opponent uses.

Another factor to consider is which plays the opponent is unlikely to run. Some coaches are very determined not to give up yardage via a loss on a perimeter play, so they concentrate instead on the inside game. While a coach may not be able to determine which plays an opponent will run, he can often get a good idea of which plays they will not run.

From The Fringe Area

Will the opponent try to score from the fringe or will he just try to drive for the score? Knowing these tendencies gives the defense an advantage. Be aware of both the offensive and defensive fringe possibilities.

Goal Line Defense

The objective of the defense is to prevent points from being scored. If the opponent's offense gets into the fringe area, the defense should try to deny the opportunity for a field goal. If the opponent gets inside the five, the objective is to mount a great goal line stand and prevent the touchdown.

As with other critical but less-frequent plays, a coach should practice goal line defense more than he expects to use it in a game in order to perfect it. Even though few opportunities exist to run plays inside the five, goal line defense must be thoroughly planned and practiced. Players should know how to adjust to every formation and to the motions that can be used in each formation.

A great benefit of goal line defensive scrimmages is the physical toughness that is developed. "They will not pass!" was the call of the 400 Spartans at Thermopylae as 10,000 Persians unsuccessfully assaulted them. One high school student body used the call "Thermopylae" to remind its team of the importance of tough defensive play. That challenge from the 600 members of the student body pushed the team higher than they would have otherwise been expected to go.

Remember that teams win with repetitions, not with tricks. Be ready and able to execute the game plan!

9

Handling The Clock

Acoach should always strive to use the clock to his advantage. The clock is important throughout the game, not just in the final two minutes. The clock is a factor whether a team is ahead or behind. When fans, players, or even coaches think of a typical "beat the clock" situation, they usually imagine 30 seconds on the clock with the game on the line. But, winners are often determined much earlier in the game.

To handle the clock effectively, the coach should have at his disposal both the plays and the collective mentality regarding how to use them. He needs plays that bleed the clock, such as in-bounds runs and safe passes. He also needs plays that stop the clock, such as out-of-bounds plays or high-percentage first down plays that require the clock to be stopped as the chains are moved. Here are some examples of situations that can be practiced:

• The offensive team is six points down and has one time-out. The defense has three-time outs, and the ball is on the offense's 35-yard line.

• The offensive team is two points down with the ball on its 20. The field goal kicker is accurate from the opponent's 25 and closer. Three minutes remain and the offense has two time-outs.

A difference of one point or one time-out can significantly alter how those last few minutes or seconds will be played. A team may find itself in a "must win" situation with

30 seconds left in the game, but it will also be in key situations near the end of the first half with the game very much in doubt. In either case, a plan for how to score and how to use time-outs is essential.

End of the Half

Situations that have a dramatic effect on the outcome of the game can often occur at the end of the first half. For example: The underdog team is ahead 10-3 and has the ball with 1:10 remaining on its own 30. This team will receive the second-half kickoff, so it will have back-to-back possessions.

If the team runs its two-minute offense and throws three incompletions, the offense will have to punt. The opponent will get the ball back with a chance to score and tie the game. In this situation, it may be better for the underdog team, even though it is playing very well, to go into the locker room ahead 10-3. Based on statistics, the team is unlikely to score from that field position, so it should protect the lead.

In another example, a team is playing defense. A minute remains in the half and the opponent has just kicked a field goal to take the lead at 10-7. How the defense finishes the first half affects how the third quarter will be played.

Two-minute situations should be practiced regularly because they occur every week and can impact the outcome of the game. A plan is needed for handling each situation, such as whether the team is ahead or behind, which team receives the next kickoff, or which team is playing with more emotion.

Consider this example: The score is tied at seven, the underdog has the ball with two time-outs, and 1:23 remains in the half. The offense understands it is best to end the half with the score tied, so play calls should keep the ball in-bounds and the players must avoid penalties during this phase of the game. If the offense happens to break a long play and winds up on the opponent's 42, the whole situation changes. The offense has added 50 yards to its stats sheet, but the yardage is meaningless unless the team scores. In this case, the offense should try to move the ball into field goal range, take the three points, and end the half with a 10-7 lead. Even if the field goal is missed, little time will remain for the opponent's offense. A team must realize how a two-minute situation can change in mid-drive, and they must learn and practice what to do when such a change occurs.

Staying with the same example, assume the field goal kicker's range is from the 23-yard line or closer. The offense now has a first-and-10 with three time-outs, and 19 yards are needed to reach field goal range. The offense should be aggressive with the ball. Short-yardage plays will take too much time, but the quarterback must not throw an interception. By practicing these situations, the team will be prepared and aware of its options.

If one play gets the ball to the opponent's 21, the coach may choose to have the quarterback take a knee on successive plays, and then kick the field goal. Time-outs still remain, however, and so does the chance for a touchdown. The scenario has changed again! The potential field goal should be protected, but a touchdown is also a possibility. In just a few seconds of clock time, both the coaches and the team have altered their plans from punting with as little time remaining as possible, to kicking a field goal, to protecting the field goal opportunity but going for the touchdown.

The offense can take an aggressive shot at scoring while still protecting a time-out to allow for the field goal. Although the quarterback sees three time-outs on the scoreboard, he understands that he may use only two.

End of the Game

Every player recognizes the most common "must win" situation that can occur near the end of a game. The team with the ball is behind by seven points or fewer. The offense must score a touchdown to win. This situation must be practiced; otherwise, the players will experience not only a huge adrenaline rush, but also a loss. The offensive coach should call the first play and have a second play already in mind. What if the first play gains big yardage? The situation has now changed, so the next play must also be different.

In another example, the trailing team gets the ball on its own 20. The defense knows the offense must drive 80 yards in two minutes. The defensive coach wants to force the offense into running a lot of plays in order to score. This "waiting game" may force the offense into an error. On the first play, however, the offense runs a draw that gains 60 yards. The defense must now be more aggressive. A blitz call would be a great choice because the offense is in hurry-up mode and might forget to look for a possible blitz.

In golf, players see many different kinds of putts. Some putts are straight, others break from right to left, and other putts break from left to right. Putts vary in length from less than an inch to seventy feet or more. In football, "beat the clock" situations occur in just as many varieties. With the ball on the 25-yard line on 20 different occasions, each situation would still be unique. In one situation, a team is ahead; in another, it is behind. A team may face a blitzing defense on one occasion and a zone team in another instance. A team might have three time-outs or none. In one situation, the offense gets a big gain on the first play; in another, a sack forces the team to change its plans.

High school teams might plan never to deviate from their core offense in the two-minute situation. Instead of sending out four wide receivers, the offense might stay in its basic I formation. Whatever the strategy, it must be planned and practiced. Practice enough of the possible situations to make the team comfortable with the idea of reacting to changing circumstances. Some form of practice on two-minute situations should take place every day in training camp. During the playing season, both the offense and the defense should practice a variety of scenarios, including the major two-minute situations. Review these situations again during walk-throughs on the day prior to the game. At any level, a great deal of thinking and practicing must be devoted to playing in top form in key situations. A well-prepared team is confident when the game is on the line.

Before the defense takes the field in a two-minute situation, coaches should summarize the circumstances for the players. With the offense in the game and ahead by one with a minute to go in the game, the defense should be reminded that the opponent has no more time-outs. Even if the offense is forced to punt, the opponent will have to throw routes to the sidelines to get out of bounds, Therefore, the defense should be in a cover-six or cover-seven zone. Remind the defense of the opponent's tendencies in this situation, and emphasize the need to avoid penalties. Stay calm and remind the defense that they have practiced this situation.

Considerations When You Must Score

If the regular offense hasn't been successful in the "must score" situation, the coach must use a scheme that gets the best scoring players on the field with plays that can win. A running offense or a balanced attack might be effective for most of the game, but a passing attack is needed when a team faces a "must-win" situation in the last few moments of the game. Some coaches follow the philosophy, "When you pass, three things can happen, and two of them are bad." However, passes and pass-related plays such as draws and screens are needed when a team must score to win with time winding down.

Many teams plan to get their best offensive people into the game for the two-minute offense. If the coach decides to put in his four best receivers, he reduces the number of blockers to six. Because the defense may blitz seven, the offense must be prepared to handle a six-on-seven situation. One approach would be to limit the number of formations and plays. However, if the offense becomes too simple, it might not be able to move the ball and score. A complex offense, on the other hand, may increase the potential for errors at the most critical point in the game.

The point differential and time remaining determine the number of yards per play that the offense must gain in the number of seconds remaining. These factors may reduce the types of plays that can be called. For example, If the offense must drive 80 yards in a minute and a half, then it has about 11 seconds for every 10 yards gained. The coach should call plays that either stop the clock by ending out-of-bounds or move the ball at least 10 yards to reset the chains. The defense is unlikely give up an easy reception on a post pattern. With about five to 12 seconds per play. the quarterback should throw high-percentage passes.

If the amount of time per yard needed is much less, the quarterback may have to throw deep curls, deep outs, trick plays such as a hook and lateral, or even a "Hail Mary.". Therefore, the two-minute offensive plan should include a variety of plays with different yardage-gaining potential.

The two-minute offense should feature pass plays that will be effective against both two- and three-deep schemes with man-to-man or zone-under coverage. With the offense expecting to see the blitz if it begins to gain yardage, the pass patterns in the plan should work against man-to-man coverage. If they are executed properly, hooks and curls also work well in this situation. Don't forget to include the short-yardage plays that are needed to cross the goal line.

How to stop the clock without using time-outs must also be included in the two-minute plan. The head coach should take responsibility for calling all time-outs in the two-minute situation rather than placing that burden on his players. Well-schooled players know they must keep playing until a time-out is called. Some coaches invoke an "alert time-out" rule in certain situations. This rule is frequently used when the team is playing defense and needs to conserve time for the offense when it gets the ball. When the opponent is trying to "bleed" the clock, the offense will run plays that keep the ball in bounds. If the opponent's play fails to stop the clock, the defense's coach decides if he wants to call a time-out. The players look to the coach as soon as the play is completed. If the head coach signals a time-out, the players run immediately to the nearest official as they signal. Since the defensive captain might be at the bottom of the pile or otherwise unable to see the coach's signal, getting a time-out called promptly is a team responsibility. It is part of the collective mentality that must be developed with the team. The "alert time-out" rule should be practiced.

When it comes to stopping the clock, certain situations require the coach to change his priorities. A quarterback sack is a good example. With a sack, even a final time-out may have to be called; otherwise, too much time will pass as players unravel, the ball is set, and the next play is called.

Coaches must also plan for the last play of the game, the play on which the team must score to win. Three plays should be determined and practiced: a play from the 15-yard line or closer, a play when the ball is between the 35 and the 15, and a play that can result in a score from farther out. The latter two plays might both be of the jump-ball, "Hail Mary" variety, with several receivers flooding the same area. On these plays, one receiver leads and one or two receivers trail the primary receivers. Each receiver is ready to play a tipped or batted pass. (Figure 9-1)

If only a field goal is needed to win, the scoring zone changes. Instead of needing to reach the goal line, the offense only needs to get within the kicker's range (usually around the 25-yard line). Since each kicker is unique, and because wind and weather affect the distance from which he will be accurate, the coach must consider these conditions as he plans his two-minute strategy and makes tactical decisions during the game.

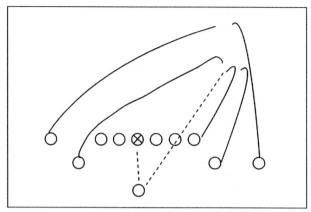

Figure 9-1. Jump ball play

Play Calling

If a coach normally sends the play in with a player, but then signals in the plays during the last two minutes, he can expect some communication problems and missed signals. The quarterback may be the best person to call the plays in critical, time-sensitive situations, but only if he is prepared to do so. Some coaches signal the formation, which limits the quarterback's choices and makes a play easier to call. The quarterback will already know whether he can use a controlled passing game or that he must throw down the field. He must also know whether a field goal or touchdown is needed, how many time-outs are available, and other key information.

Offensive Possibilities in the Last Two Minutes

• Versus man-under:

  - Use crossing patterns

  - Clear with three-deep routes and drag one man

  - Clear with two-deep routes to eliminate underneath man cover, and cross two

• Versus zone-under (5- or 6-man zones):

  - Use curl-flat combination (reading widest underneath zone), and the quick screen

• Versus two–deep, use four verticals

• Versus three-deep, attack the weak side

• Running plays

  - Use quarterback draw versus man

  - Use bootleg versus zone

Playing for the Last-Second Field Goal

A team's last time-out should be reserved for a field goal if three points can win the game. The play before the time-out should be used to give the kicker the best angle for the kick. Select a play that can position the ball in the middle of the field without risking a loss of yardage. The ballcarrier must realize his job is to get yards only in the middle of the field, and position of the ball is more important than extra yardage.

With no time-outs left, try to get the ball to the middle of the field on first or second down, and then stop the clock with the next play to allow the field goal team to get into the game.

Running Out the Clock

The quarterback should down the ball by taking a knee when the opponent has no time-outs left and fewer than 30 seconds exist for each remaining offensive down. The "kneel" play takes only about two seconds to complete. Some coaches run longer plays, such as a rollout action with the quarterback protecting the ball with both arms and sliding before he is tackled. Such a play could take three to eight more seconds off the clock, because more time would be required for the officials to move the yardage marker and spot the ball.

Each time-out called saves approximately 25 to 35 seconds. This includes the time it takes for officials to spot the ball and start the play clock, the time it takes to call the play and snap the ball, and the two to eight seconds it takes to run the play itself. Therefore, it is critical coaches on both sides of the field to know the number of remaining time-outs.

Factors to Consider in Clock Management

- Time management, communication and play execution
- Manage the remaining time.
  - Use time when ahead, either on offense or defense.
  - Conserve time when behind on offense or defense.
- Protect time outs.
  - Use if essential for a critical play-calling situation.
  - Use before a critical play, such as a game-winning field goal.
- Have a plan!

10

The Importance of the Kicking Game

With the current emphasis on special teams, the kicking game has become more important in the eyes of fans. Coaches, especially those who focus on field position, have always understood the importance of the kicking game and have emphasized it in practice. A number of successful coaches believe the kicking game is second in importance only to defense.

While fans and some football commentators talk about the breaks, coaches realize that most of those breaks come from poor or inadequate coaching by one coach, or from effective teaching and emphasis by the other coach. Most breaks in the kicking game happen because of sound coaching decisions based on well-developed plans.

A high percentage of breaks in football games occur during the kicking phase. Many coaches believe that, in close games, the losing team always seems to make at least two more mistakes in the kicking game than does the winning team. Those mistakes can include poor snaps, short kicks, ineffective coverage, a poor hold on a field goal or extra point attempt, or inadequate protection. Mistakes result in long returns, blocked kicks, wide field goal attempts, missed extra points, short punts, and other momentum-changing events. A coach who wants to make an impact in the kicking game must decide how much emphasis to put on special teams. With so many variables and possibilities in the kicking game, a coach can't focus on every factor. But, most coaches can improve their team's kicking game attack and defense.

The kicking game incorporates both offensive and defensive aspects. Punts and kickoffs are defensive plays; kick returns, field goals and extra points, and the seldom-used quick kick, are offensive special team plays.

Because of its importance, the kicking game might well have been the first impact category covered in this book. Many factors and plays take on added significance in the special teams part of the game. Examples include penalties, turnovers, big plays, red zone situations, and two-minute drills.

Statistics indicate that one of every five or six plays is a kicking play, so approximately 20 percent of the game involves kicking. How many teams practice the kicking game 20 percent of the time? Coaches should consider devoting more time to this aspect of football, because kicking plays frequently are more important than most other plays in a game. The average kick or punt involves much more yardage than the average running or passing play. Many special teams plays involve scoring, such as extra points, field goals, and possible touchdowns on kick returns or blocked kicks. Kicking game plays often result in changes of possession, and these plays can gain or lose significant amounts of yardage. A breakdown on a kicking play can turn a game around. A coach should acknowledge the importance of these potential outcomes in the kicking game and devote sufficient planning and practice time to the subject.

One statistical analysis of football games won at different levels found that the outcome of nearly 40 percent of high school and college games was determined by the kicking game. The statistic was about 30 percent for the pros. Extra points, punt and kickoff returns, and field goals are very important factors in nearly every game. When the defense gets a block or a long return, for instance, that play often breaks the game open.

Professional teams average about five punts and kickoffs per game, and they have the opportunity to return about four kickoffs and two or three punts. Coaches should review their stats to see how often they kick off, punt, and return kicks, especially in the big games. The kicking game becomes more important as the game gets closer.

Field position was more important before more teams starting playing today's popular possession-style game. With field position football, the kicking aspects of the game are much more important. As the passing game developed, the kicking game lost much of its importance in the minds of many coaches. Most coaches today would rather throw on third down rather than call a quick kick to gain field position.

It was 1969 when George Allen showed his commitment to the kicking game by hiring Dick Vermeil as the NFL's first special teams coach. Other coaches also started to see the importance of the kicking game. After all, there are three major parts of a football game: offense, defense, and kicking. Many coaches believe a team must win two of these parts to win a game. In earlier eras, coaches emphasized defense and kicking and played field position football. The idea was to keep the opponent on its own end of the field and wait for a mistake that allows the offense to move a short distance for a score.

It was the field position coaches who developed the concept of zones on the field. Each zone dictated the types of plays an offense might run and on which down to kick the ball. Knute Rockne used five equal 20-yard zones. Darrell Royal used other boundaries for his zones. Royal called the area between the 35-yard lines "the alumni zone", where his team's job was to entertain the fans. Once inside the 35, however, his team's job was to score. Other coaches labeled the zones by color. Between the 35-yard lines might be the orange zone, from the 35 to the 20 the green zone, while the area between the 20 and the goal line was known as the red zone. Only the red zone label endured as a standard used by all teams today.

Field position advocates would often punt on first down inside their 10, on second down inside their 20 or 25, and on third down inside their 35. They used the kicking game to minimize the opportunities for offensive mistakes. Tactics to improve field position included surprise quick kicks to increase kicking yardage and to move opponents deeper into their own territory. This type of kicking strategy to control the zones of the field is used rarely today. Some teams still revert to the old-fashioned field position game on rainy or cold days when the elements reduce their opponent's offensive efficiency. Bad weather produces bad footing for running backs, reduces passing efficiency, and increases the likelihood of mistakes such as blocked kicks and fumbles.

Many head coaches at the college level have assumed direct responsibility for special teams because they recognize the importance of the kicking game. Most teams devote at least a 20-minute block of practice time each day to the kicking game. Some coaches add work on the punt block, punt return, and field goal block to the defensive portion of the practice.

A famous, successful college coach once decided to take over the kicking game portion of his team's practice. He scheduled the segment to follow wind sprints at the end of practice. The assistant coaches were not needed, so they went to the showers. The coach attempted to instruct all eleven players by himself. The team already had an excellent kicker and punter, so the kicking game was adequate. The head coach would have seen significant improvement, however, if he had included kicking game work in every practice and involved the assistant coaches in the effort.

Theories differ on whether to play substitutes on special teams or to place the best players on the field. Especially at the high school level, Mom and Dad will be just as proud to see their son play a down or two on offense as they would be to see him on the kickoff team.

A coach who decides to emphasize the kicking game must be able to teach the long snap, the hold, the field goal kick, the kickoff, the punt, and the onside kick. Rarely-used plays such as the pooch punt and squib kick should also be taught and practiced. The coaching staff should also to teach the blocking techniques needed for each type of kicking play, and the coverage lanes and tackling techniques needed. The team must learn and practice how to block a kick. Once the coach can teach these fundamentals and the assignments needed for each type of kicking play, he must consider the options available for each type of play and choose those that fit his team. Each week in his scouting analysis, the coach looks for chinks in the other team's armor that will allow his team to block or return a punt, kick away from a dangerous return man, plan a fake kick, or return a kick for good yardage.

Be Aware of the Opponent's Special Team Standouts

Scouting to make special teams more effective is critical. During the team's first meeting of the week, the coach should point out the key performers on each of the opponent's special teams. Identify the best return men, the best cover men, and the best kick blockers. Before covering the opponent's kicking schemes, make players aware of the big-play special teamers on the other side. The coach should present a plan to neutralize of the opposing players who are most likely to affect the kicking game. The whole squad should be alerted to these potential game-breakers. An effective motivational tool is a challenge to the special teams to focus on a single standout player and prevent him from affecting the game. Alerting players to the danger of a particular opponent can make them play with even more desire; a dynamic performance is often the result.

Self-scouting is also important in determining how the special teams performed in a game. Who made the tackles? Who blocked the kick? Who made effective blocks on kick returns? The next step is to recognize special teams' performances. Use charts to show how effective the special teams have been in previous games.

The Kickoff Game

If a team's kicker can kick the ball through the end zone on every kickoff, then the coach might spend less time on kickoffs during practice. Most teams don't have that luxury; therefore, a number of approaches have been created to improve the effectiveness of kickoffs.

If the opponents have a great returner, kick away from him, or use a squib kick that bounces along the ground and allows the cover players to converge before the return can be set up. Another approach is to employ two kickers with different skills. Use a strong-legged kicker for deep kicks; let the more versatile kicker execute the squib kicks, cross-field kicks, and pop-up kicks into open areas.

Team Approaches to Kicking Off Deep

The basic kickoff play puts the kicker in the middle of the field with five tacklers on each side of him. (Figure 11-1) Many coaches use other alignments to increase the effectiveness of the play. Some teams kick the ball from a hash mark, rather than the middle of the field, in order to reduce the opponent's options for a return. It is certainly more difficult for a team to return a kick to the opposite side from which it was caught. Every step the ballcarrier takes toward the far sideline gives every member of the kicking team a one-step advantage and reduces the chances of a successful return. On the other hand, if the returner stays on the same side of the field as the kick, then each defender has a narrower lane to defend. (Figure 11-2) College rules require at least four players on each side of the kicker. High school rules have no such restriction. (Figure 11-3)

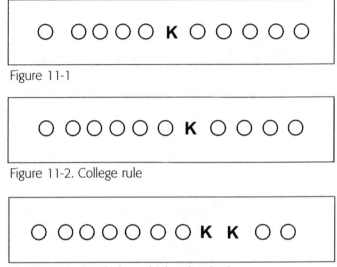

Figure 11-1

Figure 11-2. College rule

Figure 11-3. Two kickers—high school rules

Some coaches place one or two players farther back than the kicker so they get a longer and faster run toward the receivers. One of these men usually is a "wedge breaker" whose assignment is to dent the four- or five-man wedge of blockers that protects the returner.

Some coaches use two kickers in certain situations: One kicker is set up to kick deep to one side of the field. The other kicker's role is to kick to the opposite field or to execute an onside kick.

Many soccer-style kickers can kick the ball into the end zone with remarkable consistency. A touchback is certainly the ultimate goal of kickoff strategy. Likewise, a kicking team is at a disadvantage if it doesn't have a kicker with a powerful leg. Two solutions to this problem are the squib kick and the pop-up kick into an open area.

To squib-kick the ball, some kickers will lay the ball on its side instead of teeing it up. The kicker strikes the ball off-center to cause it to take uncontrolled bounces. It takes longer for a squibbed kick to get downfield than it does for an airborne kick, so the coverage is closer to the ball than usual when it is caught. A squib kick is also more likely to be fumbled.

Another shorter kick is the pop-up kick. It can be aimed at an open area of the field or at a lineman who is more likely to fumble the ball. In general, kickers tee this ball with the top of the ball slanted downfield.

Deep Kickoff Technique

For the deep kickoff, the objective is to kick the ball consistently inside the 10-yard line with a hang time of four seconds or more. The effectiveness of the kick depends on both distance and hang time. Both factors help the cover people to advance farther into the opponent's territory. The soccer-style kick usually travels farther because it allows more of the foot to get into the ball, which transfers more force and focuses more power behind the ball. The soccer-style approach also allows for a longer leg swing, which produces more speed and transmits the added force to the ball.

In order to take the proper number of steps, the soccer-style kicker usually starts about 10 yards behind and five yards to the side of the ball. The straight-ahead kicker should start about 8 to 10 yards back. The exact distance should be determined by having the kicker start at the tee, run back toward his goal line until he feels comfortable, and then kick an imaginary ball. The coach marks the spot, and the kicker repeats the exercise several times until his run at the ball seems comfortable. This method is used to determine the setup and proper number of steps for kickers who use either style.

In most cases, the kicker tees the ball as straight as possible. Some kickers have individual preferences regarding how the ball is placed. There are practical reasons for altering the ball's position on the tee. A soccer kicker who wants to eliminate a hooking kick, for example, should point the top of the ball away from the hook. A hooking kickoff is not always a problem, by the way, because it can be very difficult to catch—especially if it bounces.

As the kicker approaches the ball on a kickoff, he generates more speed than he would with a field goal attempt because he is taking more steps. His strides are also longer and his kicking leg travels along a wider arc, and this motion also contributes to additional leg speed.

For soccer-style kicks from a two-inch tee, the kicker's foot plant should be located six to eight inches to the side of the tee and two to four inches behind it. With a one-inch tee, the toe should be two to four inches in front of the ball. The ball should be kicked just below its center. As the ball is kicked, the hips and shoulders should be parallel to the goal line.

If the ball hooks to the left (for right-footed kickers), the plant foot is probably too close to the ball. If the flight of the ball slices to the right, the foot is probably too far from the ball.

For straight-ahead kickers, the plant foot should be about four inches to the side of the ball. For kicking the ball off the grass, the plant foot should be eight to 10 inches behind the ball; for a one-inch tee, the distance should be about 12 inches; and for a two-inch tee, the plant foot should be about 14 inches behind the ball. The higher the tee, the greater the height and hang time of the kick. Contact should be made just below the center of the ball. A lower contact point means more spin on the ball and a higher trajectory, both of which result in a loss of distance.

If the kicker is aiming toward a certain area of the field, such as away from a dangerous returner, then he should follow he ball into that area after the kick. Because kickers often represent the last line of defense on a kickoff, they must learn to tackle.

The kicking motion is the same for a kickoff as it is for a field goal attempt. However, power is more important than accuracy in the kickoff, so the kicker should attack the ball with a very quick leg action. A kicker should get his whole body behind the kick. Some kickers, in fact, lift their bodies as much as two feet off the ground as they follow through on a kick. They should then land on the kicking foot.

The Squib Kickoff

Coaches use a squib kickoff for two main reasons: Either they don't have a kicker capable of getting the ball deep into the opponent's end, or they want to minimize the possibility of a big return. Squibbing a kick toward one side of the field is the simplest way to alter the kick return plans of a team that likes to use the wedge. Since it affects the return team's timing, the squib makes it more difficult to set up an effective return. The kick will be short, but the ball will be difficult to control and may be fumbled by the receiver. The kickoff team must be alert to the possibility of a loose ball.

Techniques for the Squib Kick

The objective of the squib kick is to keep the ball away from the better returner, to make it bounce unpredictably, and to kick the ball hard enough to get it inside the opponent's 30-yard line.

The kicker should tee the ball and strike it on the top half to make it take a number of high and low bounces. The kicker may also set the ball on the ground at various angles to the line of scrimmage. The kicker should experiment to find the best ball placement and the best contact point.

If the ball is placed with the ends perpendicular to the sidelines, the best spot to kick it is an inch off-center and halfway up the ball. Kicking the ball on its bottom half imparts backspin, which causes the ball to rise and reduces distance. also In addition, the ball may not bounce crazily when it hits.

The Onside Kickoff

The onside kick is actually an offensive play, because the kicking team is trying to regain possession of the ball. As an essential part of the kicking game strategy, the onside kick need not be reserved for desperate, game-ending situations in which the team must get the ball back to score and win. A well-executed onside kick at an unexpected has an excellent chance to be successful.

Some coaches use the onside kick on 70 percent of their kickoffs or more. Their thinking is that with a 30 to 50 percent chance of recovering the ball, it is worth the risk. Even if the kick team fails to recover the ball, the opponent has gained 10 to 20 yards more than a normal return.

One high school team in Los Angeles used the onside kick about 90 percent of the time and recovered about half of those kicks. The team's normal kickoff coverage would stop the return team between the 30 and 35, and even if it didn't recover an onside attempt, the ball would end up near the opponent's 45. If the kicking team recovered, then its offense started at the opponent's 45. With nearly a 50 percent recovery rate, this team's strategy paid off in most cases.

Some coaches threaten the onside kick on every kickoff. One formation that makes this strategy effective is to place every player on the kickoff team close to the kicker. If the kicker kicks the ball straight ahead 10 to 15 yards, then the kicking team will have eleven players near the ball. The kicking team can either execute an onside kick or the players can return quickly to their normal position for a deep kickoff. If the receiving team comes up close to stop the onside kick, the kicker can kick the ball to an area of the field left vacant by the receivers.

The onside kick can be executed from a regular kickoff alignment. In obvious onside kick situations, however, most of the cover men line up near where the ball will be kicked. For most onside kicks, the ball is placed on one hash mark and kicked to the wide side of the field.

The assignments of the cover men include those who will block the receivers, those who will attempt to recover the ball after it has gone 10 yards, and a "fielder" or stopper who will be near the sidelines to stop a kicked ball from going out of bounds.

Techniques for Onside Kicks

In one commonly-used technique for an onside kick, the kicker strikes the ball close to the top. This causes the ball to bounce low along the ground at first, and then to bounce high into the air. The ball should be kicked between the up men on the return team or toward the sideline, 12 to 15 yards deep. Kickers should experiment to see what angle of the ball on the tee works best for them. Some kickers like the ball to lean as much as 45 degrees toward them.

The dribbler kick is another type of onside kick. The kicker approaches the ball at full speed, but then he kicks it hard enough to carry only 12 or 13 yards. This kick is effective against teams that either align their front people 13 to 15 yards deep or have the front retreat as the kicker approaches the ball. The dribbler kick should also be aimed between the up men on the return team. Blockers should be assigned to the up men on the receiving team, and they should be reminded that no member of the opposing team may be touched before the ball has traveled at least 10 yards.

Another type of onside kick is a high kick toward the sideline and 13 to 15 yards deep. This kick is effective against teams who align their up men close together in the front line. The high sideline kick should be placed on a hash mark and kicked to the wide side of the field. The kicking team should have a "stopper" whose job is to make sure the ball stays in bounds.

The scouting report should indicate the alignment, quickness of retreat, speed, and dexterity of the up men on the opponent's kickoff team. Players who are accustomed to handling the ball should be used on the kickoff team and positioned to be near the ball. The more onside kicks a team has in its playbook, the better its chances of recovering one.

A team may also have two kickers on the field on a kickoff team. The kicker on the right side of the formation handles the right deep kick and onside kicks to the left. The other kicker lines up on the left side of the formation; he is responsible for the left deep kick and all onside kicks to the right.

Another technique for executing an onside kick requires skill and practice. The kicker strikes the ball in the middle, but off-center, to impart sidespin. When this kick is performed properly, the ball travels about 10 yards toward the opponents, then it begins to spin back toward the kicking team. The ball moves like a top along a semicircular path.

Kickoff Coverage

Covering the kickoff is another important element of the kicking game. Every kick coverage scheme includes two men who are responsible for the outside. In addition, one or two players usually act as safeties. The other seven or eight men attack the ballcarrier in one or two waves. They maintain coverage lanes about 4 to 5 yards wide so the ballcarrier cannot easily go around them or run through a gap in the wave. (Figure 11-4)

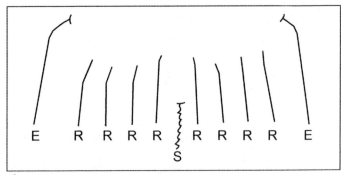

Figure 11-4

Some teams employ "wedge breakers" who attempt to break through the wedge of blockers that protects the ballcarrier until he finds a gap in the coverage and runs for daylight. Other teams attack the gaps between the wedge blockers with a cover man for each gap.

The kickoff team may also use players designated as linebackers or safeties. Some teams use one safety, usually the kicker, while others use two. Some kickoff teams play one or two linebackers slightly behind the group of wedge breakers; they may also use one or two safeties.

Cover players must stay in their assigned lanes as they run down the field. If all players were to run directly to the ball, they would open a hole in the defense for the returner to exploit. The lanes start out about five yards apart but reduce to three or even two yards as defenders get closer to the ballcarrier.

The kickoff team must defend the entire field until the return play is recognized. Whether the return is a wedge, trap, or another play, the defenders reduce their lanes and converge on the ball as the return team commits to a strategy. A good scouting report should indicate where to check for a potential blocker. Since most teams drop their blockers back before attacking upfield, blockers are usually easy to identify. A simple head fake or an adjustment of the cover path can move the blocker out of his base position. The cover man can then cut back into his proper lane. If the blocker can be forced to stop his feet or cross his legs, then he can be eluded easily by the cover man. The cover man might not even touch the blocker, but the cover man should be prepared to ward off an attempted block

Because some teams target specific coverage men to be blocked on the return, many coaches instruct their rushers to cross as they run downfield. In most cases, the return team assigns numbers to the men on the kicking team. Many return teams pay particular attention to the ends on the kickoff team, and they run traps and other blocking schemes to neutralize them. Crossing the end and one or two other men can disrupt the blocking assignments of the return team.

Coverage Assignments

Coverage assignments vary depending on whether the situation calls for a deep kick, a cross-field or squib kick, or an onside kick. Against a team that employs the wedge, assign a man to each gap between and outside of the wedge blockers.

A 50- to 55-yard kickoff should have a hang time of at least 3.9 to 4.0 seconds. The cover players need that much time to get close to the opponent's 30-yard line. The returner should catch the ball between his own 10 and 15. Defenders should get their first shot at the ballcarrier between the 15 and 25, depending on the height and length of the kick.

As the kickoff team sprints down the field, players should be focusing first on maintaining their lanes, then on making the tackle. Recall that kickoff lanes start about five yards apart and close to two yards or less as players approach the ballcarrier. One player, usually the kicker, remains behind as the safety. Not all coaches use the 10-man charge on kickoffs: some coaches position seven to nine players in the front group, followed by one to three backers a few yards behind. (Figure 11-5) The second line of cover people must break down, reduce their lane responsibilities, and then look for the tackle. They must be ready to stop the ballcarrier if he passes through the wedge.

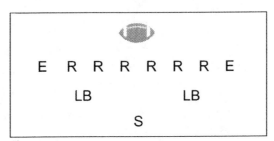

Figure 11-5

Some coaches prefer a more cautious approach to kickoff coverage. While the first player or players to get downfield may take a full-speed shot at the ballcarrier, the others break down about five yards from the ball in order to cover more area from side to side. Each defender must strive to keep the ballcarrier from getting around him to the outside.

Many methods exist to assign routes and responsibilities to the kickoff cover people. If the opponent uses blocking assignments rather than a wedge, cross different kickoff team players to try to confuse their assignments. Crossing the outside two, three or four men might be effective against a team that likes to trap the outside man or men, but a well-disciplined return team will adjust to this tactic. Using two sprinters is more likely to cause problems for the return team: The sprinters can take different paths on each kickoff, and their speed makes them difficult to trap. When the returner heads to the sideline to take advantage of the trap, the expected opening should be filled by one or both sprinters.

Contain

Contain men are responsible for throwbacks and reverses. When returners cross, either to execute a reverse or to fake one, the contain men should be taught always to tackle the man coming toward them.

Individual Techniques

Cover people must run at full speed while avoiding potential blockers. The first thing the cover man must determine is where the ball is headed. A quick glance upward by a cover man before he encounters a blocker should help him in locating the ball. A look downfield at the returners will give a cover man a good idea of where the ball will be caught.

Individual coverage techniques require cover men to carry out a variety of assignments, i.e., attack the ball, contain, play safety, block, or recover the onside kick. Since most players on the normal kickoff are required to attack the ball, they must recognize how to get to the spot where they can attack. If a player meets a blocker far ahead of the ball, then he should use a finesse move to avoid contact. The cover man should work to get the blocker off-balance or stopped. A head fake, a cut behind, or using his arms to ward off the block can all be effective tactics. The cover man should get back in his lane as soon as he passes the blocker.

As the cover man encounters a blocker near the ball, particularly in a wedge, he must attack the ball through the blocker. A quick fake might shift the blocker's weight or focus. The defender attacks with the shoulder nearest to the ball. Either the hands or the shoulder can make the initial contact. It is essential that the defender keeps his head up so he can always see the ballcarrier. The first line of attackers should maintain their speed and attempt to tackle the ballcarrier or force him to alter his path. The first defenders to get downfield should go for the all-out big hit. Even if he doesn't make the tackle, an aggressive, big-hit player can alter the return man's path and reduce the effectiveness of the wedge. If a cover man must attack through the wedge, he should either find a gap or try to occupy blockers.

If contacted by a blocker, a cover man can use pass-rush techniques to slide past him. Hitting with a hand shiver in the chest, or using a club and swim or a rip, can free the cover man from the blocker's hands or shoulders. A hard shoulder block against a wedge blocker can put him off-balance and help to penetrate the wedge.

Kicking Off After a Safety

Even though safeties occur infrequently, kicking off after a safety must be covered in practice. A punter may be used to punt the ball on this free kick down. The ball must leave the punter's foot before he crosses the line of scrimmage. The cover people won't get quite as much run as they do with a normal kickoff, so the danger of being offside is greater. The likelihood of an offside penalty can be minimized by coordinating the movements of the punter and the kicking team during practice.

Coin Flip: Kick or Receive?

Most teams prefer to receive the kickoff if given the choice, but strong defensive and kicking teams often choose to kick the ball instead. The strategy employed by these teams is to hold the opponent inside its own 30-yard line, force a punt, and then take over somewhere around their own 40-yard line. In certain situations, a team might choose which end zone to defend in order to take advantage of the wind. A strong wind at the back might be much more valuable than taking the first possession of the ball.

Scouting Considerations

- What is the opponent's receiving formation?

- Check opponents' numbers to determine who plays where.

- Which front men are good targets for onside kicks?

- What types of returns do they run?

- If they use a wedge, do they set it in a specific place on the field, or do they set it on the ball wherever it has been kicked?

- Who is the best return man?

- Where should you kick deep kicks?

- Should you squib?

- How can the cover people avoid their blockers?

- Can the surprise onside kick be used against them?

Situations to Practice

- Cover lanes

- Cover men avoiding blockers

- Onside kick, when expecting an onside kick and when surprised by an onside kick

- The squib kick

- Kicking off after a safety

12

The Kickoff Return

As he prepares the kick return team, the first priority the coach should cover is the onside kick. The players must plan for it, learn to recognize its variations, and practice how to respond when an opponent tries it. Next, the coach must decide how much time to spend on the kickoff return portion of the team's playbook. The simplest kick return strategy is to form a wedge and try to get the ball out to the 35-yard line. The wedge strategy will even produce long returns on occasion. A more aggressive coach draws on a wider variety of plays in an attempt to score on every return. Some examples of creative kick returns include running a trap from behind a traditional wedge; cross-blocking the five inside players on the kickoff team, and then running a wedge through the cleared area; or setting individual blocks timed to clear the ballcarrier for big yardage.

A wedge return can be run to the right, middle, or left part of the field. Other returns might involve trapping the outside or double-teaming the middle. The coach should, at a minimum, have specific plans for attacking coverage teams that are disciplined to stay in their proper lanes and those cover teams that converge quickly on the ball. Against a kickoff team trained to defend the lanes, a wedge can be effective. Kickoff teams that get to the ball quickly can be attacked with traps or wall plays.

Because the kicking team is sprinting and the return team's players know where they are going, kickoff returns are relatively easy to execute, but the coach must decide how much time to devote to this part of the game. A great defensive team might not want to devote a lot of time to just one or two returns per game. If a team is returning an average of four or five kickoffs per game, however, it should definitely be working on kickoff returns.

Defending the Possible Onside Kick

If a kicking team is prepared, it may try an onside kick on any kickoff. Knowledgeable coaches generally look for the chance to gain an advantage if the odds are in their favor. The front line should always be ready for the onside kick, and they should work on it weekly in kickoff return segments.

The onside kick is being used much more often today than in the past as coaches see its advantages. Therefore, the return team should not give a smart coach an advantage by retreating too quickly or not being ready for the onside kick.

Defending the Certain Onside Kick

How does the opponent execute a desperation onside kick? Few teams have more than one play for this situation. More return players must move up if an onside kick is expected. At least two players should stay back, however, in case the kicker kicks the ball deep from the onside kick alignment. If the coach expects an onside kick, then he should put the "hands team" in the game. This group is made up of those players who are accustomed to handling the ball. The coach should also position the return team so that nine or 10 players are near the restraining line to maximize the chance of recovering the ball. A common approach is to kick the ball about 12 to 15 yards deep to the opposite sideline. With this type of kick, the kicking team will send a stopper to keep the ball in bounds. Someone on the return team should be assigned to block the stopper so he can't get to the ball. If the ball goes out of bounds, the receiving team gets great field position. If an opponent likes to kick between or into the front line players by using a dribble kick, the receiving team should practice recovering this slow, rolling kick.

Returning the Deep Kickoff

A kickoff can be considered a success if the kicking team keeps the ball from crossing the opponent's 25-yard line. A kick return is a success if the return team advances the ball to its own 35 or beyond.

Kickoff return tactics involve a wedge block, cross-blocking, double-teaming, trapping, or setting a wall of blockers on one side of the field. These tactics are also used in combination. Refer to figures 12-1 through 12-5 for different types of returns.

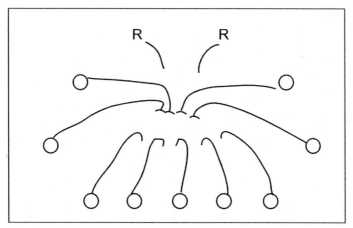

Figure 12-1. A double wedge return

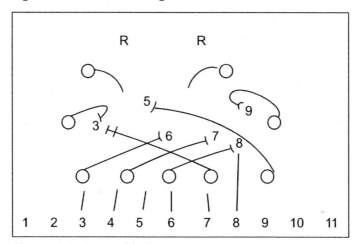

Figure 12-2. A cross block return

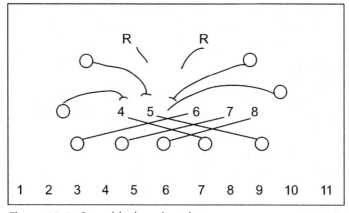

Figure 12-3. Cross block and wedge

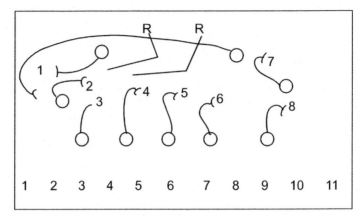

Figure 12-4. A trap on the end

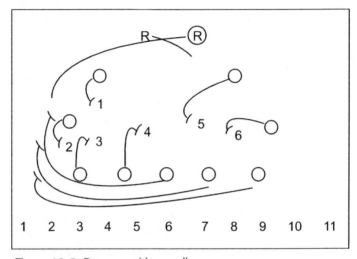

Figure 12-5. Reverse with a wall

The kickoff return play gives coaches the opportunity to use special trick plays such as the reverse, fake reverse, or the long lateral pass. Another example is the notorious "bubble play," in which the receiving team huddles around the ball before the kicking team members have a chance to get downfield. At the signal, the return team breaks the huddle and all players act as if they have the ball. The kicking team must figure out who has the ball before anyone can tackle him. The bubble play is not the most effective play in football, but it certainly is fun to practice. The play was more effective when it was invented more than 80 years ago. The first "bubble play" coach had a leather oval, which simulated a football, sewn on each jersey. You can imagine the confusion among the tacklers.

Kickoff Return Theory

Some coaches' primary goal in returning kicks is to get the ball out to the 35. Others coaches want to score. Desired objectives determine the types of returns used and the amount of time devoted to practicing the return package. If a team is looking to score, three factors work in their favor. First, no other play finds a defense so completely spread across the field. Second, in no other play can pursuit be reduced as effectively. Third, in no other play can defensive reactions be predicted as well as on the kickoff. For teams that have effective kicking schemes and practice them well, the yardage rewards are greater than those produced by any other offensive play. The team should be told that the kickoff return is their best offensive play, and then the team should practice returning the ball three days a week.

The return scheme for most teams is a simple wedge. The timing of the blocks is not a major factor, and when it is executed effectively the wedge has a good chance of getting the ball to the 35. A team may score with this play, but it is not a preferred choice for teams who want to score on kick returns. The cross-block, trap, double-team, or combination schemes are used by teams that want to score on the return.

Some coaches like to cross-block the middle five or six cover people, and then form the wedge behind those blocks. Other coaches start a wedge but trap behind it. Some teams use a simple trap on the widest man. Another popular tactic is to work the middle with one to three double-team blocks to open a lane for the returner.

The Returners

One of the safety men should have the responsibility to call "me" or "you" when he determines the ball's direction. If the ball is kicked over the heads of the safety men, they must still get back to cover the ball because it is live. If the return team downs the ball in the end zone, it is a touchback and the ball is placed on the 20. The kicking team can recover the ball in the end zone for a touchdown. On all kick returns, the returner should be moving into the ball as he makes the catch. This simple move can add an additional three to five yards to every return.

Blocking Timing and Technique

In any return scheme, blocking is the critical element. The rule that prohibits blocking below the waist is the reason for the popularity of the wedge return.

Some coaches simply have their blockers retreat a given distance, five to 25 yards from where they lined up, and then turn to meet their assigned cover men or set a wedge. If the wedge blockers retreat to the same spot on the field each time, and let the ballcarrier come to them, play timing is simplified. Other coaches have their wedge players retreat to within 10 to 15 yards of the ballcarrier, and then turn and block. This tactic provides additional protection to the ballcarrier but it also changes the timing on the blocks.

For a traditional cross-block wedge, the wedge center should set up about 12 yards from the returner. The set of the wedge depends on the direction of the kick. The wedge center should be in front of the ball but no wider than the numbers (for a college team) or the inbounds line (for a high school team). When the wedge has formed and the returner has the ball, he should yell "Go!" and the wedge should move forward. The other four people in the wedge set up a yard apart and block straight upfield while staying in a line.

A tougher but more effective blocking scheme has the blockers retreat until they are 10 to 12 yards from the ball, and then make their blocks. In order for this approach to work, it must be drilled until the timing becomes precise. The blockers must retreat while reducing their cushion, timing the blocks so they occur 10 yards from the returner. A blocker must swivel his head first to see the returner, and then to see his man, and he must recheck his position about every 10 yards. The block is very simple, but the timing is difficult. This approach works very well on a trapping return. It also works on a middle return, especially if the cover men stay in their proper lanes.

Nearly any contact with a cover man will set him off stride and allow the returner to get past him. The following block pays great dividends if players practice it enough. For a team that uses both right and left returns, the blockers must practice blocking both ways. Always use a returner in your blocking drill. The ball does not have to be kicked. The coach signals the cover man to start downfield; about three or four seconds later, the coach signals the ballcarrier to start forward. When the ballcarrier is 10 to 12 yards from the ball he yells "Go!" This cue signals the blockers to make their blocks. No blocks should be made before this verbal signal. The block, by rule, must be made in the front. The blocker drives both hands into his opponent's chest. The downfield arm strikes the mid-chest while the other hand drives up under the armpit or under a near edge of the shoulder pad. A yell just before the block often causes the opponent to turn his chest toward the blocker as he reacts to the yell. After contact is made, the blocker must work his body toward the area he is protecting. During this time, the blocker must take care to avoid penalties. A clip on a kick return happens far more often than it should. It is nearly always spotted by an official and it's a mistake that can be minimized by coaching proper blocking position and technique.

The blocker must realize that the man he had when he numbered off before the kick is his man, no matter what cover lane that man takes. Many teams count the kickoff team from right to left without numbering the kicker, who is likely to be the safety. Sometimes the kickoff team crosses men or motions them behind the kickoff team, and then sends them sprinting downfield in different lanes from those in which they started. These motioning players may vary their lanes from week to week, but some teams keep them in the same lane each week.

If the plan is to double-team, such as in a middle return, one player should protect the area of the return while the other protects the runner by blocking the cover man from the front. If performed correctly, these blocks occur nearly at right angles to each other. The block from the side should precede the block from the front. (Figure 12-6)

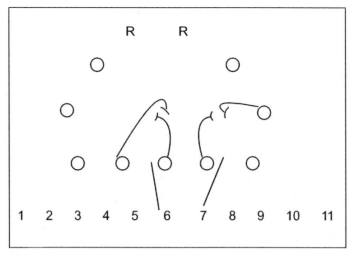

Figure 12-6. Double team drill

Some coaches prefer to set a wall on the right or left side. Runners can be held in their lanes by running a reverse or fake reverse, with the ball ending on the predetermined side and the ballcarrier being protected by the wall. The crossing action of the returners should hold the cover people in their lanes until they know where the ball is actually going. Good faking is essential.

The right, middle, and left returns utilize the timing blocks made 10 yards in front of the ballcarrier. The ballcarrier starts up the middle on all three returns. When he gets to within 15 yards of the nearest cover man, he yells "Go!" No blocks should be made before his signal. On a middle return, all blocks can be made on this signal. (Figure 12-7)

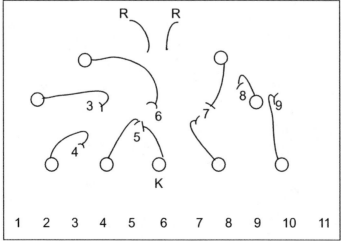

Figure 12-7. Middle return

If the return is right or left, the ballcarrier cuts at a 90 degree angle toward the sideline. If he cuts at less than a 90 degree angle he risks cutting inside the widest tacklers, who will be inside their blockers. The wider blockers must delay their blocks until the ball is within 10 yards of them. The ballcarrier cuts upfield about 10 yards from the sideline and works to about five yards from the sideline. At this point, the player assigned to the widest cover man on the return side traps him out. However, if the defender takes an inward angle instead of containing, he should be blocked in. The second widest cover man on the return side should also be blocked in. Some teams cross their two outside cover people to confuse this block. Therefore, the return team members responsible for blocking these crossers must be drilled to make either the inward block or the outward trap.

KICKOFF RETURN ASSIGNMENTS

Diagram 12-8 is an example of how a team with three returns might summarize blocking assignments for the players for kickoff returns to the left, middle, and right. The kickoff team is numbered one to eleven from the return team's right to left. For the blockers, the number on the left is the assignment for a left return, the middle number is for a middle return, and the right number is for a right return. (Figure 12-8)

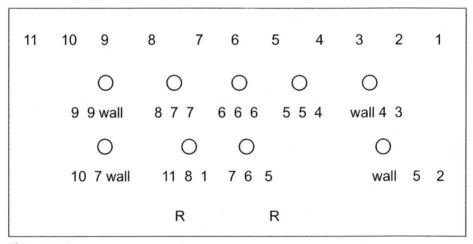

Figure 12-8

Situations to Practice:

• Defending the certain onside kick

• Defending the surprise onside kick

• Returning the squib or onside kick

• Returning a kickoff after a safety

Things to Remember:

• If the kickoff does not travel 10 yards, then the receiving team has the option of taking the ball where the play ended.

• A kickoff is a live ball after it has gone 10 yards. The kicking team should recover any ball that has gone 10 yards. In college and professional football, if a ball goes into the end zone and is not downed by the receiving team, it is still a live ball and can be recovered for a touchdown. In high school, a ball kicked into the end zone is dead.

• On a kickoff the kicking team may catch the ball in flight after it travels 10 yards.

Scouting the Opponent's Kickoff Game:

• Chart the game kickoffs for distance, direction and hang time.

• Note the personnel on the kickoff team and determine who has speed and who is eager to make the tackle.

• Note which player or players are the safeties, and how far back they hang.

• Do the players stay in lanes or converge? Who comes down the fastest?

• Do they cross any players, and if so, who?

• Do they have a couple of very fast people who may start in motion early and cross other players' lanes? How can these players be handled?

13

The Punting Game

Many coaches believe the punt is the single most important play in a game. Whether the punter or the snapper is the most important player in a punt situation is a matter of debate.

In order to minimize mistakes by the punting team, the coach should have the team practice live punting every day. In addition to overall special teams work, the coach should schedule a specific portion of each practice to punting. Fewer punts will be blocked or returned if the punt is emphasized in practice.

The Long Snap

The long punt snap is one of the most important skills in football. It is often difficult to find a good long snapper. Professional teams often draft a lesser player if he is an effective long snapper. Legendary coach Paul "Bear" Bryant estimated that 98 percent of blocked punts occur because of a poor center snap. Every coach should try to make certain that he has at least two excellent snappers on his squad.

The long snapper does not have to be a center. Some teams use a reserve quarterback or anyone else who can get the job done. Many teams use the spread punt formation, which puts the punter 12 to 15 yards back. By rule, the snapper can't be hit with his head down, so the snapper need not be an effective blocker, but he must be able to deliver the ball quickly and accurately. The long snap should travel 10 yards in .6 to .7 seconds, 13 yards in .75 seconds, and 15 yards in .8 seconds. Delivering the snap with this speed requires strong latissimus dorsi, lower chest, and triceps muscles.

Snappers should be timed from the first day of practice, or from the day they start snapping in the off season. Teach them to focus on speed and a low trajectory. It is far better to have a fast snap that bounces than a high snap that makes the punter jump. With practice, however, a good snapper should be able to avoid both the high snap and the low, bouncing snap. The snapper has only one job: Make a perfect snap.

Long Snapper Techniques

In the snapper's stance, his feet should be a good distance from the ball so he can reach out comfortably. By reaching for the ball, the muscles are stretched; as all physical educators know, a stretched muscle is better prepared to react. The snapper's feet should be even, with the toes equidistant from the line of scrimmage. If one foot is back, the snapped ball may drift to one side. Most of the weight should be on the balls of the feet, with little weight placed on the football.

The snap can be made directly from the ground or by lifting the ball and then snapping it. The snap from the ground is the fastest and most preferred method. The snapper grips the ball with his dominant hand as if to throw a forward pass. The last two fingers usually grip the laces. The snapper's other hand may rest on top of the ball to aid in direction control. The ball should be nearly flat on the ground; lifting the nose of the ball can cause an error in the snap. With both hands on the ball as it passes between the snapper's legs, errors that would change the ball's trajectory are minimized. A one-handed snap is more likely to produce such errors.

Good snappers can put the ball right where the punter wants it every time, even under pressure. The punter should provide a target by placing his open hands just inside the knee of his kicking leg. The reason for this seemingly-low target is that the great majority of poor snaps are high snaps. If the snapper aims at the punter's knee but his snap is three feet to high, then the snap still reaches the punter at shoulder height. The snapper would have to miss the target by six feet or more in order to snap the ball over the punter's head.

Many punters give a target at chest or shoulder level. If the snap is two or more feet above that target, then the punter must reach or jump to catch the ball. This additional action throws off the timing and might delay the punt long enough for it to be blocked. An extremely high snap that flies over the punter's head will travel up to 20 yards behind him and will result in about a 60-yard loss for the punting team.

When to snap the ball should be the snapper's decision. The punter may yell, "Set!" when he and the team are ready. If a defensive team is trying to stunt through the center's area to block the kick, the snapper should be alerted to this fact by a guard if the snapper fails to see the oncoming stunt. The snapper should look around for a possible stunt near him, then get ready to snap the ball, and then snap it.

The snap should travel quickly to the target. Most snappers raise their hips just before starting their backward snapping movement. This upward hip action signals the punt blockers and allows them to get a jump on the snap. Therefore, a snapper should learn to minimize his hip movement prior to the snap. The snapper's follow-through should point directly at the target with both arms. Snappers who use only one hand often deliver the ball off-center. Right-handed snappers, for example, often snap the ball to the kicker's left. By resting his left hand on the ball and following through, a right-handed snapper can deliver straighter snaps.

The snapper should keep his eyes on his target until the ball has left his hands. The palms of the hands point upward as the follow-through is completed. The snapper must follow through with both arms. Only after the ball is released should the snapper bring his arms forward and raise his head as he looks for someone to block. The snapper blocks passively, if needed, as in a pass protection block. If he finds no one to block, the snapper releases downfield toward the punt returner. The other players in the punt coverage set their lanes based on the path of the snapper.

Developing Snapping Strength

To increase snapping speed, long snappers should use the lat pull-down machine in the weight room. Instead of pulling the bar down behind his back in a traditional lat exercise, the snapper should grip the cable with both hands and pull down with his arms straight. In all strength development work, specificity is desired, i.e., an exercise should simulate as closely as possible the actual movement being strengthened.

Snappers can improve their speed by providing manual resistance to each other, and the following exercise can be just as effective as working with weights: Players A and B face each other. Player B grasps players A's wrists. As player A simulates snapping the ball, player B provides resistance. Use maximum resistance to develop strength and lighter resistance for more arm speed and power. Power is a combination of strength and speed. Power can also be increased by having the snapper use a heavy ball, or by attaching a surgical rubber tube to the ball and snapping against that resistance, or by tying a rope to the ball and having another player provide resistance as the snapper drives the ball backward.

Recent research indicates the importance of increasing strength not only in the specific muscles involved in an action, but also in those muscles that affect the posture of the action. Although working muscles against resistance with the body standing (such as with a lat machine) is effective, it is more efficient for the snapper to work the same muscles from his snapping position. On many weight machines the snapper can assume his normal snapping position and still work on strength or power development. A low pulley, found on most Universal-type machines, or a rowing machine would offer effective exercises. The snapper should work on improving speed and power on the low pulley, and use greater resistance in standing exercises to develop his strength.

Long Snapper Drills

Snappers can practice at home by painting a six inch-wide target on a wall about two to three feet above the floor. The snapper should practice from the distance required in a game. If the snapper is weak, he should start closer to the target until he is confident and can snap hard and low.

The very best snappers can put the laces just where the punter wants them. While it is more important to have the laces in the correct position on a field goal play, it also helps on punts. of the snapper should be consistent in aligning the laces before every snap. If he delivers the ball with the laces in the same position every time, then a pre-snap adjustment should allow him to snap the ball to the punter with the laces where the punter wants them.

No matter how small the team, it is wise to have three players for each essential position. A team should have three quarterbacks, three punters, three holders, three placekickers, and three long snappers. There is no time, for example, to teach long snapping to an inexperienced player on the sideline if the starter is injured. At the amateur level, having at least one essential-position player per class means the team is covered in case of a key player's injury, illness, or ineligibility.

Punting Techniques

The punter sets up 10 yards behind the line of scrimmage in a tight punt formation, at 12 to 14 yards for a high school spread punt, and at 15 yards for a college or pro spread punt. Shoes and other equipment can make a big difference to a punter. Hip pads should not restrict his movement. He should wear low-cut shoes to allow for maximum ankle extension. Some punters remove the tongue of the shoe and kick without a sock because they do not want shock-absorbing materials between the football and the bones of the foot. Punters usually tie their shoes on the inside so there is no knot where the ball makes contact with the foot. Punting barefoot reduces the shock-absorbing material between the ball and the foot and it allows for maximum ankle extension. The barefoot technique is more important as a psychological factor, however; it does not have a significant impact on the punt itself.

In punt position, the punter should be standing with feet parallel or with his kicking foot slightly forward. His feet should be shoulder-width apart and his weight should be on the balls of his feet. He should be ready to move right or left to catch a bad snap. The punter's hands should give the snapper a low target just inside the knee of his kicking leg.

Unless they have been instructed to give a low target, punters usually provide a target at chest or shoulder height. A small error in the height of the snap can be disastrous by throwing off the punter's timing and by increasing the likelihood of a blocked punt.

The mechanics of the punt start with the punter moving in front of the ball. If the ball is snapped to his right, for instance, he steps right with his right foot and then moves his left foot to re-establish his stance. A punter should never reach to the side for the ball but always move his whole body in front of it.

If the snap is over the punter's head, he should try to step back and reach up for it. If is the ball is still out of reach, then the punter must turn and run to get the ball. After he gets the ball, the punter should run away from the defenders and try to find an open spot from which to punt the ball. If he has no opportunity to kick the ball, the punter should run with it.

With a good snap the punter looks the ball into his hands. As he takes his first step, he adjusts the laces either straight up or perhaps an inch to the right if he is right-footed. Both the laces and the valve are "dead spots" where the foot should not strike the ball. The punter's foot drives halfway into the ball on contact, and the ball rebounds faster off the foot if it is more compressed. Kicking a dead spot reduces the amount of compression, which reduces distance.

The punter keeps the ball out and away from his body from the catch to the kick. He should not bring the ball in close to his body. The punter can hold the ball as high as the chest or as low as the waist.

The grip is important. Most coaches teach punters to place the kicking-side hand near the back of the ball with the other hand forward and on the side of the ball. Some coaches prefer the hands to be under the ball and to slide out on the drop. Most coaches prefer to have the kicking-side hand on top of the ball to minimize the possibility of additional contact after the drop. With a hand under the ball, the releasing hand may pull the ball with it to the outside as it releases, or it could tilt the nose of the ball too far downward.

Most punters angle the ball slightly inward and downward to improve the spiral of the punt. The inward angle should position the front end of the ball over the big toe or slightly outside it; experience teaches each punter the correct angle for him. A few coaches prefer punters to point the ball directly upfield with its longitudinal axis bisecting the laces of the shoe. This placement often results in an end-over-end kick that bounces farther than a spiraling punt.

The number of steps taken may vary from punter to punter. The one-step punt is unlikely to be blocked, but it may not generate maximum distance. The three-step punt is comfortable for many punters and it may increase the distance of the punt, but it is easier to block. The two-step punt is a good compromise.

The following instructions refer to right-footed punters. The traditional two-step punt begins with the feet parallel. The punter catches the ball, and as he takes a long right step he adjusts the ball so the laces are on top. He follows with a long left step and drops the ball as the kicking leg begins to move forward.

Some coaches start punters with their left foot back. The first step is still made with the right leg, but it is shorter because the left leg is behind. This action is quicker and doesn't bring the punter quite as close to the line of scrimmage.

The second step, taken with the non-kicking leg, is a long step. During this second step the ball is held at a height between the waist and the chest. Beginning punters often hold the ball too high or even toss it upward. Every inch that the ball falls increases its speed and usually increases the drop of the nose of the ball. In windy conditions, a longer drop is affected more by the wind.

The three-step punt can be used if the punter is 15 yards back. Many of the best punters use this method. The punter takes a medium to long step with his non-kicking leg, then a long step with his kicking leg, then another with his non-kicking leg. The final step and drop are the same as with the two-step kick. The three-step punt requires four to four-and-a-half yards as the punter moves toward the line of scrimmage. Therefore, the punter must be 14 to 15 yards deep at the start of the play.

As he waits for the snap, the punter's head should be down and his eyes on the ball. Near the end of the last step, the kicking leg starts forward. The punter drops the ball during the forward whip of the kicking leg. His body must continue to lean forward. The punter should drop the ball with the belly of the ball on or just outside the instep. The outside drop produces a better spiral.

The drop is the most important part of the punt. Without a perfect drop the ball will not hit the foot correctly. The punter should experiment with the several methods of holding the ball so he can drop it with accuracy and consistency. The primary objective is to drop the ball as short a distance as possible. The longer the ball is in the air, the more any mistakes in the drop are magnified. As mentioned previously in this chapter, wind also affects a longer drop more than it changes a short drop.

A correctly-dropped ball, if it hits the ground, should bounce back just to the outside of the kicking foot. This is a way to test the correct angle of the ball. Have the punter drop the ball on the ground and see if it bounces just to the outside of his kicking foot. The ball should be dropped from a spot above where the kicking leg will swing.

Many kicking coaches use a soft chalk, such as gymnastic chalk, to mark the bottom seam of the ball. After the kick, the chalk should leave a mark on the shoe across the midway point of the laces. The mark should point slightly inward toward the big or second toe. Check to see which angle of the ball gives the most effective punt, then work to make that drop consistent.

A punter with a quick leg can drop the ball from a lower point. A punter with a slow leg must drop it from a higher position in order to get the ball to his foot at the proper spot.

For a higher punt, the punter holds the ball higher and closer to his body. For a lower punt, such as one into the wind, he holds the ball lower and farther from his body.

If the ball is dropped correctly, the nose will drop earlier than the rear of the ball. This ball position is correct as the ball hits the instep. The ball should be at the same angle downward as the angle of the instep. A correct drop and foot contact will result in a spiraled kick.

If the nose of the ball is too far down or the toe is up at contact, the ball may fly end-over-end as it spins backwards. This ball action produces a short punt that will probably bounce back toward the scrimmage line after it hits. If the ball is not angled downward sufficiently, the punter may strike the rear tip of the ball with his ankle. This produces another end-over-end kick, but in this case the ball spins away from the punter.

The kicking phase starts with the kicking leg back. As the leg whips forward through the ball, the kicking foot is extended so that the top of the foot continues in a straight line from the lower leg. For most punts, the ball should be contacted just below knee level to produce good height on the punt. The contact point should be higher in cold weather; the ball will not compress as much, so it will leave the foot more quickly. The forward tip of the ball should be one to two inches ahead of the toes.

The height at which the ball is contacted determines the trajectory of the ball. If punts are going high and short, then the contact point is too high. In addition, a higher contact point reduces contact time between the ball and the foot. The kicking leg may also be nearly fully extended if the ball is met too high. Both of these factors affect the amount of force imparted to the ball.

The follow-through should be as high as possible. If the kicking leg stops quickly, then the leg was slowing down as the foot struck the ball. This action reduces the speed of the ball. A punter must be flexible in order to execute a proper high follow-through.

The force of the kicking action tends to give the body a rotating motion and forces the kicking leg to finish on the opposite side of the body. This motion must be minimized for maximum efficiency. Soccer-style placekickers, when asked to punt, often follow through across their bodies.

A hang time greater than four seconds is essential for good punt coverage. Some punters achieve hang times of more than five seconds. An excellent hang time for high school punters is 3.8 seconds; for college punters, 4.3; for pros, 4.5. An acceptable hang time would be .1 seconds per yard from the line of scrimmage. In other words, a 38-yard kick should have a hang time of 3.8 seconds.

Individual differences among punters account for some variation in technique. A punter with shorter arms should hold the ball closer to its end. A long-armed player may hold it more in the middle. A punter with less ankle flexibility may need a greater angle of the ball to the foot so that the toe does not contact the ball and create an end-over-end punt.

Wind requires adjustments to the kicking action. Kicking into the wind requires the punter to stay low, lean forward, and meet the ball at a lower point to keep its trajectory down. Kicking with the wind requires a higher kick. Meeting the ball higher, perhaps as high as mid-thigh, produces a higher ball flight.

Strength and Flexibility for the Punter

The punter should be a good athlete. The leg speed necessary for kicking is, to a large degree, a genetic blessing. But, the punter's natural ability can be greatly increased with effective exercise. Punters should do the splits with the kicking leg forward. This stretch should be done at the end of practice when the player is loose. It will probably take months before his pelvis can actually touch the ground. The stretch is important because tight connective tissue in the hamstrings, the back of the hip, and the back of the knee can slow down the punter's leg before the ball has left his foot. The punter's foot should follow through over his head. Only this level of flexibility allows maximum force to be transmitted to the ball.

The punter should also be able to extend his foot downward such that the front of his shin and the top of his foot form a straight line. This ankle flexibility can also be developed. Olympic divers, who also need that straight line of the leg and feet, often tie their feet to a board to stretch. Some divers have been known to sleep with their feet tied to the board.

A punter should also work on strength and power in his quadriceps, hip flexors, and abdominals. A weakness in any of these areas will reduce his power.

Working on a low pulley, or with a rope tied to the ankle with someone giving resistance from behind, will increase strength and power in the punter's hip area. Normal curl-ups or crunches will strengthen the abdominals. A leg extension machine will strengthen the quads. If no machine is available, the punter can sit on a table with his lower legs hanging over the edge. As another person provides resistance against the ankle, the punter tries to raise his leg.

Practice Bad Snaps

To practice bad snaps, the punter should stand with his legs shoulder-width apart in a bent-leg, ready position. This stance allows him to move right or left to get in front of an errant snap. The punter should not reach for a wide ball, but move in front of it. During punting practice, the coach should alert the center to snap where he is directed. At least once during every punting practice, the coach should signal the snapper to snap a ball a few feet to the right or left so the punter learns not to be surprised when he gets a bad snap in a game. Snaps that force the punter to jump, as well as higher snaps that the punter cannot catch, should also be practiced. When a snap goes over the punter's head, he must turn and run, get to the ball, and then turn to his kicking-leg side to make the kick. Even when he is practicing alone, the punter should toss the ball to himself in different spots and with the laces in varying positions. This exercise helps the punter get used to moving his body to the ball and adjusting the laces as he moves forward in his kicking action.

Time of the Punt

A punter must kick the ball quickly; an acceptable time frame is 1.2 seconds from the time the punter catches the ball until it leaves his foot. The total time between the snap and the punt depends on the distance from the snapper to the punter. At 12 yards, the punt should be away in 2.0 seconds; at 13 yards, 2.2 and at 15 yards, 2.3. If the total time is .3 seconds longer than the times stated above, the punt will probably be blocked if the opponent is rushing the kick. In general, the total time for a punt in a game is shorter than in practice because the snap is faster and the punter kicks more quickly.

On every punt in practice, make certain that the punter calls the direction and height of the punt so it is second nature in a game. "Right-high" or "middle-middle" calls help the cover people locate the ball more quickly.

The Punt Team

Now that the essential techniques have been covered, let's get to the play itself. Many coaches believe that the punt is their most effective offensive play. Not many plays average 35 to 40 yards.

Depending on the skill of the punter, the coach may decide to work on high, non-returnable punts. It is always a good idea to make the receiver move before he catches the ball. The more variables the returner faces, the greater his chances of making a mistake. If the sun is behind the punter, for example, the ball should be kicked so that the receiver must look into the sun. Adding one more variable to the receiver's concerns—which might already include the sun, wind, distance, height, and pressure—could result in a fumble or a long roll if the returner decides not to pick up the ball. In order to avoid surprises, the cover team must know where the ball will be kicked.

In designing a punt play, the coach must be concerned with the protection of the punter, the direction of the kick, and coverage of the kick. The best protection would be very tight but that would reduce the effectiveness of coverage. The best coverage would place the kicking team members far apart, but that would reduce protection of the punter. Therefore, a happy medium must be achieved.

In high school and college, kicking team members may release to cover the kick at any time. At the pro level, only the widest two players may release immediately. The others must wait until the ball has been kicked.

Directional Punting

More of today's coaches consider directional punting as part of their strategy. With this type of punt, the punter kicks the ball away from the returner and forces him to run a considerable distance to retrieve the ball. Because the returner might not get to the ball before it hits the ground, a directional punt increases the chances for a fumble. If the ball hits the ground, the punt team may gain additional yardage on the bounces. In directional punting, in fact, a punter should consider kicking the ball lower so that it hits the ground sooner and gets longer bounces. Lower punts require that the ball be contacted earlier in the punter's leg swing. In certain instances, a coach may decide to punt out of bounds 35 or 40 yards upfield.

Punt Formations and Coverage

Many punting formations exist, and all can be modified by varying splits in the line and by spreading the ends or keeping them tight.

The spread punt formation is still quite common. It was the first movement away from the tight formation that provided maximum protection but poor coverage. With line splits of two to three feet and backs in the center-guard gaps, blocking rules are inside-on-outside. The personal protector lines up about five yards deep and the punter is positioned 12 to 15 yards deep. The punter's depth depends on the abilities of the snapper and the punter. The ends may be lined up tight (within three feet of the tackles) or split out. Professional coaches are more likely to spread the ends because the rules allow only the ends to release before the kick. (Figure 13-1)

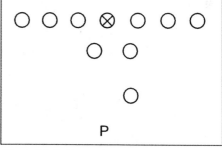

Figure 13-1. Spread punt

The old tight punt formation allowed for maximum protection, so the punter could kick from only 10 yards deep. But, effective punt coverage was very difficult. As the importance of coverage became recognized, the tight punt gave way to other types of punt formations. The tight formation is still used, however, especially when a team is kicking from its own end zone. (Figure 13-2)

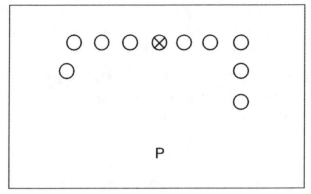

Figure 13-2. Traditional tight punt

The tightened spread formation is used by spread punt teams that are kicking from their end zones, and by teams that must punt from closer to the line of scrimmage because they have no strong snappers. The punter is positioned 12 to 13 yards deep.

Many teams put the upbacks in the wing position. This variation allows for a quicker release and assigns the lighter, quicker backs to protect the flanks. Ends may be tight or spread. This alignment also works well for passes when the punt is faked. In this formation, the line and wings usually take 2 steps back on the snap; this move reduces the effectiveness of defensive stunting. The tactic is effective at the professional level because the inside people may not release until the kick is made, but in high school and college it slows the punt coverage considerably. (Figure 13-3)

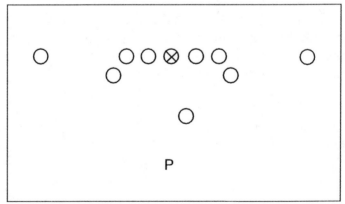

Figure 13-3. Wing punt with ends split

A punt formation that offers good coverage with only seven players, and provides maximum protection, is the three man back (semi-spread) formation. With three line-men back, it becomes very difficult for the return team to block a punt. (Figure 13-4)

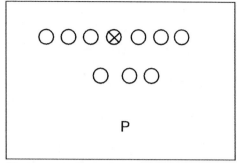

Figure 13-4. Three men back semi-spread punt

Punt formation with motion can free a man for a pass on a fake punt. Motion can also help a wide cover man avoid being bumped by the return team. (Figure 13-5)

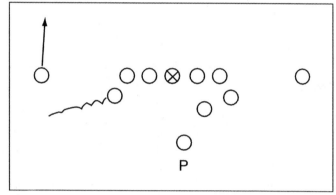

Figure 13-5. Wing motion

Punt Protection

Punting is difficult under normal situations. When the opponent rushes 11 men because it has to block the punt to have a chance to win, the odds of executing a successful punt can be discouraging. A new punt protection cannot be drawn in the dirt as the punt team takes the field. If the punt team is prepared, however, the coach can say, "Hey guys, look for the 11-man rush. Now let's go kick it!" Punting against an 11-man rush should be practiced during training camp and at least once a week during the season.

The punt team should also practice punting out of its own end zone with maximum protection at least once a week in practice. Some coaches add extra players to the defense when practicing the punt. They might put 14 or 15 people on the rush team. The other 11 defenders can still work on the return if the coach allows only the extra players to rush.

In man protection schemes, the first thing that linemen and protecting backs must do is determine which man they must block. The personal protector should call out the front (six- to 11-man rush), and then call out the side that is overloaded. If necessary, he can even give extra directions such as, "Joe, help left!" Some coaches have each player call out the number of the man he will block, while other coaches tell players to point to their men. Knowing these blocking assignments eliminates confusion and lets the backs know who they should block. Overloads can be identified and the blocking scheme adjusted if necessary.

Man blockers use a pass protection technique to keep rushers from getting inside. A blocker must be aggressive, however, because for every yard he drops back, he has an extra yard to go in his cover route. In punt protection, the interior linemen should be taught to hold their men for two seconds (1001, 1002), while the outside people may be able to release after blocking for one full second. Man protectors don't drop back because it puts them further from the returner. The personal protector must also take care not to back up, or he may block the punt. The backs should hold their blocks until they hear the sound of the punt.

In a formation that uses up-backs, instruct the backs to check inside to outside if they find no immediate defender to block. If no defender leaks through to the inside, up-backs should check each hole and pick up the widest rusher if no other rusher threatens the punter.

If a defender is obviously holding up a blocker because his team is setting up a return, that blocker can release because he has no rusher to block. There is no sense in having both the offensive and defensive people trying to hold each other up. Someone should be fighting to get somewhere, and that someone should be the punt team.

The correct blocking technique for punt protection is to pop the hands into the defender's chest while keeping the body inside or in front. A good blocker can delay two rushers by popping each in the chest with different hands. This technique can be practiced in a drill with two defenders on each blocker, with and without a live punter.

Punt Coverage

While the first essential is to get the punt off, it is also important to prevent the returner from reducing the punting team's net yardage via a big return. One or two players will probably be able to go on the snap. In high school, the cover people should have nearly six seconds to get to the returner, based on a 2.2-second punt and a hang time of 3.5 seconds. The snapper, who is usually not a blocker, can also release immediately. Some coaches hold all other players until the players hear the thud of the kick. Other coaches release players to coverage after counting off one or two seconds. In college, with a normal 2.2-second kick and a 4.3-second hang time, the cover people have about 6.5 seconds to run 35 to 45 yards and make the tackle. Do not put any player on the punt team who runs slower than a 6.5 in the 40.

Since it is common for teams to have two levels of coverage (immediate and delayed), the first man or men to get downfield can go all-out for the tackle, but they must avoid being hit by the ball in flight. The resulting penalty would be interference with the opportunity to make a fair catch. An early attack on the returner can force him to take a lateral move that slows his return and makes him an easier target for the first wave of cover people.

Once a second level player has released, he should get into his assigned lane to contain the return. He should never follow a man wearing his own color. If the player is unsure about the proper path to take, he should remember the tip, "Wider is better." Most coaches strive for lanes that start five yards wide and constrict to about three yards within 10 yards of the ballcarrier. Potential tacklers should break down about five to seven yards from the returner and be ready to move laterally. The ball should be kept inside unless the assignment is to be "on the ball."

The punter-safety man should check for a wall being formed by the return team, and then he should call out the wall's location to his teammates. The safety man should position himself on the sideline side of the return team's wall so he cannot be blocked back into the middle of the field.

Cover players should practice stopping a ball that is bouncing back toward their punter. They should also be drilled on surrounding a ball that is still moving and stopping it just before it touches the goal line.

With punt coverage, one or two men usually get to the ball almost immediately. A second wave that includes the center, guards and tackles will be five or 10 yards behind the first men. The second-wave players must stay in their proper coverage lanes. Two players will be designated as "ends" or contain men who can stop any wide plays or reverses. One or two safety men round out the coverage team.

With timed releases, one to three players leave on the snap; others, such as the contain men, can go after one second; the next wave can go after two seconds; and the last players go when they hear the thud of the punt.

Another coverage pattern sends the center and both wide players immediately to the ball. The guards, tackles and wings make up the second wave, and the personal protector and punter serve as safeties.

As with kickoff coverage, cover players must sprint to the ball. The first one or two players can try for a quick tackle, but the others must break down and maintain their balance so they can make sure tackles.

Punting Toward the End Zone

Since the object of the punt is to gain as many yards as possible, punters avoid kicking the ball into the end zone. Statistics are kept on how effective punters are in starting their opponents inside the 20-yard line.

To place the ball inside the twenty, punters either kick the ball out of bounds as close to the goal line as possible, or they "pooch" the punt on a high trajectory toward the opponent's 10-yard line. The covering team attempts to let the ball bounce toward the goal line but not ro cross it. If the returner signals for a fair catch, players should continue sprinting. The first man down should run past the returner and get in position to down a punt that goes over the returner's head.

Angling the punt to the "coffin corner" requires the punter to turn his body toward the target after he catches the ball. The punter should aim at the pylon on the side of the field to which he is kicking, adjusting for wind and any drift he may put on his punts. Many right-footed punters, for example, tend to drift the ball about five yards to the right.

A lower punt usually carries straighter to the target and is affected less by wind. A skilled punter might excel at delivering both low kicks and high hang-time kicks.

One way to practice aiming punts is to put one or two markers on the ground (pieces of white athletic training tape will do). The punter checks these marks as he makes his steps. The markers should be placed on the spots where the punter's feet should land as he steps into the punt.

The pooch punt is aimed down the middle. It may be fair-caught by the receiver or downed by the punting team. The pooch punt is easier to teach, especially if the punter is not a specialist and has limited time to practice his kicking. The punt is kicked high to allow the coverage to get down under the punt and either force the fair catch or down the ball before it goes into the end zone. The ball should be held with the nose up and kicked with the toe up to increase the likelihood that the ball will bounce straight up after it hits the ground.

Cover people should be taught to down the ball or to bat it back if it is bouncing near the goal line. Coverage should be ready to down the ball if it goes over the safety's head. Make sure the cover players know the receiving team has the option to take the ball at any spot where it was touched. Touching a punted ball does not kill it; it must be held until the official has blown his whistle. This rule is particularly important when kicking into the area between the 20 and the goal line.

An alert returner can pick up the ball and run after it has been touched by a punt cover man who failed to down the ball. Even if the ballcarrier fumbles, his team can take it at the first spot of touching, so he has nothing to lose.

Kick Return Tackling

As with any other skill, tackling a kick returner takes practice. A good tackling drill, which can be performed in "thud" mode (without taking the ballcarrier to the ground), begins with two cones set six to 10 yards apart. The kick returner starts eight yards away from the tackler. The tackler stays in front of the returner's hips, moving laterally with the returner's moves, and then makes the tackle. This drill is also effective for defensive backs. (Figure 13-6)

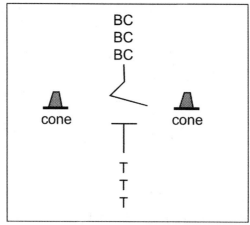

Figure 13-6. Kick tackling drill

When Do You Punt

Punting on third down might sound like a stupid idea in today's game. With high-powered offenses, a third-and-20 can still be converted. If the skill level of the passers and receivers is lower, however, there may be times when a coach should consider kicking on an earlier down, especially if his defense is strong. Today's teams often decline to punt on fourth down when they are behind but on the offensive side of the 50. If they make the first down, the drive continues; if the play fails, however, the opponent has a real advantage. Some coaches seem more enamored by fairy tale possibilities than to the realities of the odds.

If a game is being played in the rain, the ball will be slippery and soggy. This situation is not ideal for ball protection. The coach may consider kicking on an early down and letting the other team make the errors. If the ball can be kept dry, on the other hand, a wet field is ideal for passing because defensive backs must deal with unsure footing. The kicking game may also become more winnable, because slushy footing will slow the punt rushers and take away the elusiveness of the punt returner. The punt, therefore, makes even more sense on a wet field than a dry field.

Know the Game Situation

In some situations it might be best to punt the ball out of bounds, or wide to the right or left. If there is a bad snap, should the punter fall on it, or should he try to kick it or run with it? If the bad snap is in the end zone, should the punter take the safety? A safety is preferred if the punting team is ahead by three points or more, and it may be considered even when the team is ahead by two: A chance to win in overtime is better than giving up a likely touchdown and losing.

Kicking long is not always the answer. A shorter but higher kick with no return usually results in better net yardage than a long kick with an effective return. Kicking into the end zone reduces the net by 20 yards. Such a kick is the coach's fault if he has not taught the pooch kick and coverage or the out-of-bounds kick. A collective mentality between the coach, the punter and the cover people is necessary in these situations.

The most effective punts are those that are downed inside the 10-yard line. Remember to practice the situations that can cause you to win. There should be very few times in which players face a situation that comes as a total surprise because it has not been practiced.

Fake Punt

It takes real courage to run or pass on fourth-and-10, but it is necessary in some situations. As with any other play, if the coach wants to use the fake punt, then the team must work on it or it will not be successful. A play that is part of the regular offense and uses starting offensive players increases the chances for a successful fake.

Fourth down fake punts can make or break a game. If the play fails, a loss of 35 to 40 yards is the result. When a team is behind by six points with two minutes to go and has the ball near midfield, this is not a good time to try to fool the opponent. The teams that have always exploited the fake punt play are those that use their kicking game as an important part of their offense. If a team has punted on third down before, the next punt formation on third down will send the opposing safety scurrying back. A quick pass to the safety's vacated area would have an excellent chance for success. It doesn't take much practice to snap to an upback and run a sweep. If a quarterback is the upback, an option is a good call.

An opponent's punt return team may feature a number of weaknesses that can be exploited by a fake punt. Do the linemen hit and then immediately revert to their punt return blocking responsibilities? If that is the case, then a run nearly anywhere could work. Some coaches give their punters the option to throw to a wide end if he is uncovered. This play should be practiced often; it often results in a big gain.

Many teams incorporate the fake punt into their punting plans. The fake isn't called in the huddle, but determined by the setup of the return team. The deep back checks the defense, then he calls out a code word that tells his teammates whether to run the fake punt-pass, the fake punt-run, or to punt the ball. The punt is one situation in which the coach has a pretty good idea of the defensive plans: who will be aligned where, whether they will be rushing or holding up the cover people, and whether they have one or two safeties deep. No defensive situation gives the offense more options than a punt defense. The fake punt still might fail, however, and a loss of 30 to 40 yards would be the likely result.

The Quick Kick

Advocates of the field position strategy are strong proponents of the quick kick. These coaches might call the play on any down. Possession coaches seldom use a quick kick, perhaps reserving it only for third-and-long situations. Since most of today's coaches adhere to the possession strategy, the quick kick is rarely seen in modern-day football.

The quick kick can often net 60 yards with no return, while a punt is more likely to get 30 to 35 yards. In terms of yardage, a quick kick is equivalent to two or three more first downs. In addition, the safety might fumble the ball, or a defender who is inexperienced as a return team member might commit a clip or other infraction.

Several techniques can be used to execute a quick kick. From a shotgun formation, a rocker-step technique can be used. The right-footed quarterback starts with his left foot and takes three backward steps. He shifts his weight forward onto his right foot, steps with his left foot, and then kicks the ball.

In another quick kick technique, the quarterback pitches to the left halfback for an apparent sweep. On his second or third step, the back drops the ball on his right foot with the ball pointed somewhat upfield, then he kicks it soccer-style. The ball should bounce end-over-end for good yardage.

Other quick kick techniques have included a direct snap to the fullback between the quarterback's legs, or a pitch back to the fullback as he takes the rocker steps described in a previous technique. All quick kicks should be kicked low so they bounce a long way after they hit the ground.

Teams that use a quick kick often have a fake quick kick as well. They start a quick kick play motion to force the safety to retreat, then they throw a pass in the safety's area.

Special Situations to Practice

• Punting from your end zone

• Punting toward the goal line (from the 35, 40, 45, 50)

• Punting from each hash mark

• Covering a fair catch (in the field, near the goal line)

Weight Training Exercises

For The Snapper:

• Straight arm pull downs on the lat machine

• Snapping action on a low pulley

• Straight or bent arm pullovers on the bench

• Snapping a small medicine ball or a weighted football

For The Punter:

• Leg extensions on quadriceps machine for the leg snap

• Hip flexions on a high bar with the kicking leg as high as possible (with straight legs and with knees bent)

• Kicking action on a low pulley (Figure 13-7 and 13-8)

Figure 13-7   Figure 13-8

• Abdominal curls

• Flexibility work:

  - Ankle extension (work to make the ankle extend back as far as possible)

  - Splits with the kicking leg forward to stretch the connective tissue in the lower groin and the back of the thighs

- Sitting toe touches to stretch the connective tissue in the hamstrings and lower back

Drills

For The Snapper:

• Passing the ball overhand (overhead) with both arms

• Snapping at a target (a manager or a fence)

• Snapping ball and quickly assuming blocking position

For The Punter:

• Bad snap drills (signal the snapper to make a bad snap once every day during punt practice)

• Timing the punt with a snapper (2.0 seconds or less if 13 yards back) and without a snapper (1.2 seconds or less)

• Angling for the sidelines (aim at the five-yard line if right-footed punter is punting to his right; aim at the 12-yard line if right-footed punter is kicking to the left "coffin corner")

• "Pooch" punt to the 12-yard line

• Ball drop drill (the punter drops a ball without kicking it; the ball should bounce up and to the outside if the ball was dropped properly)

14

Punt Defense: Blocks And Returns

Punt defense includes returns and blocks, combination plays, and defense against the fake. Some teams work hard on fake punts and will take advantage of any weakness in the punt defense. Thus, the punt defense should have assignments for both the fake punt-run and fake punt-pass possibilities.

Most coaches give primary emphasis either to blocking or returning punts. Some teams try to block nearly every punt. Some teams try to return nearly every punt because it is so difficult to block a punt, and because the potential exists to rough the punter and give the punting team 15 yards and a first down.

Alignment

Many teams use a 10-man front with a single safety. A 10-man front provides the best chance of both blocking the punt and holding up the cover people. If the punting team splits two ends to cover, then two defenders must cover them. Many teams employ the split end with inside slot or wingback alignment for their punts. Each of these players must be covered in case of a fake. Coaches who look to exploit every possibility in the kicking game offense will throw to these players if the defense fails to cover them.

Some coaches prefer to put a defender on the potential receiver to draw his block and play man-to-man. Other coaches pull two or three players off the line just before the snap to play a zone defense against the fake. Coaches must always assume that opposing coaches can detect any weakness in the punt defense plan and may try to exploit it.

The Punt Return

In most cases, a team attempting to return a punt tries to hold up the tacklers on the punting team. Most pro teams double-team the two wide men on the punt team since they are the only two players who can leave at the snap of the ball. This rule does not apply at the high school and college level, so all potential tacklers should be delayed. Some return teams block only those opponents on the return side of the field so more of their own players can get into the return wall.

The longer the coverage is held on the line of scrimmage, the greater the opportunity for a successful return. Because a bad snap or fumble is always possible, at least one defender should rush the punt. Therefore, nine players on the return team are assigned to hold up the punting team cover men. If return team players release too fast to get into a wall, however, it will be difficult for them to defend a fake punt. On many occasions a punter has observed the eager defenders running to set up a wall, tucked the ball away, and run to the opposite side of the field for big yards.

If the punter kicks the ball high with good hang time, the tacklers have a better chance to cover the punt. Since it takes about two seconds for a kicker to deliver a punt, and most good punters hang the ball up for about four seconds and kick it 35 to 40 yards, the punt coverage team has about six seconds to cover 35 to 40 yards. Since most special teams players run a 40-yard dash in five seconds or less, there is little chance for a return unless the coverage is held up for at least two seconds.

Once the punting team members have escaped their blocks, the receiving team members will set up for the return. Most teams form a wall of players on one side of the field. Most teams choose either the wide side of the field or the side to which the punt is likely to drift.

In order to make the wall wide enough to outflank the cover men, most coaches instruct some or all blockers to run past the same point to its outside. This point is usually located near the defensive end's original spot or perhaps 5 or 10 yards wider. Some coaches put the spot on the hash mark, while others place the mark several yards farther downfield to stretch the wall. Making players run around a given spot puts the wall blockers in a better line with more effective splits between them. If they ran directly downfield from where they lined up, they would probably be too bunched and unable to create the wall effect needed for a good sideline return.

A wall blocker's job is to prevent defenders from penetrating the wall on his side closest to the returner. The blocker must make a block only if can get his head in front of the potential tackler and hit him in the chest with his hands. A 15-yard block in the back penalty destroys a punt return. Blockers must try to stay on their feet and they must recover quickly if knocked down. If a blocker knocks his man down, he should stay with him to keep him down and out of the play. If a blocker loses his man, he should sprint toward the returner to help where he can.

A safety should never line up deeper than the 10-yard line, because a ball kicked over his head there should go into the end zone. Safeties must be taught that they can't signal a fair catch and then block an oncoming cover man. In fact, many coaches tell their safeties not to make a fair catch signal unless they intend to catch the ball.

Some return teams keep two safeties back. Of course, this reduces by one the players available to rush and to play fakes. Some teams that use two safeties always cross them, with the planned returner moving toward the forming wall. For this play, the safeties know which man will end up with the ball even though they do not know who will catch it. The play will call for the safety who catches the ball to either hand it off to the other safety on a reverse, or to fake the reverse and keep the ball. Other teams teach the receiver to run to the wall while the other safety blocks the first man down the field on coverage.

One safety should always call out who should take the kick. The non-catching safety tells the returner whether to fair catch or return, depending on how quick the coverage people are coming.

The returner should catch the ball with his feet planted securely. After the catch, he starts upfield and breaks to the sideline if a sideline return has been called. The return-er can dodge a man coming at full speed much more easily than one who has a good angle as the returner heads toward the sideline. The return man must also be taught to break the first tackle. He needs to be tough in his first steps in order to fight off the first defenders who reach him. The returner should never concede yardage. Doubling back to escape tacklers gives the cover players more time to get to the ball and to pursue it effectively.

Catching the Kicked Ball

The returner should move in the direction in which the punter steps. If he is trying to kick away from the safety, the punter's steps give the safety a head start on the ball. The returner should watch the ball leave the punter's foot, and then move quickly to the spot where the ball will come down on his nose. He should notice whether the ball is high or low, spiraling or end-over-end, or anything else about the ball's flight. The returner must learn to adjust to the kicked ball, especially the high kicked ball. The ball often carries farther than expected; an inexperienced returner may misjudge the ball and let it go over his head. If the nose of the ball hasn't turned over, the ball will be short and will often drift in the direction of the punter's kicking leg. If the ball turns over, it will carry longer than expected and will often drift away from the punter's kicking leg.

Coaches must teach returners how to catch punts properly. The returner must get in position, move into the ball, plant his feet, and catch the ball with hands up and fingers open as he brings the ball into his body. His elbows should be in; if he misses the ball with his hands, he can still cradle it with his arms. Kick returners should always be working when the punters are working. They can never get enough practice catching punts or kickoffs. Emphasize getting in front of the ball, moving forward as the catch is made, and proper hand and arm position. After the returner has looked the ball into his hands and put it in the proper carrying position, he should be moving forward and ready to dodge the first man down.

The returner should catch the ball with his hands, and then move it to the ball-carrying position in the crook of his elbow with his hand cupped over the end of the ball. Only after he has secured the ball should the returner look upfield and start to run.

The returner's first responsibility is to catch the ball. If he fumbles, the kicking team is likely to recover it. This mistake results in a 35-yard gain or more for the kicking team. If the returner lets the ball go over his head, the kicking team may gain another 10 to 20 yards on the kick. Once he has caught and secured the ball, the returner may head upfield and try to gain additional yardage for his team. Above all else, however, he must catch the ball.

If the ball goes over the safety's head, he should not attempt to pick it up while he is moving in the same direction as the ball. He should get behind the ball; then, if there are no defenders near him, he can pick it up and run. The returner should use this technique in all but two situations: First, if the punting team has already touched the ball, the return man should do whatever it takes to try to gain maximum yardage because his team has the option to take the ball where it was first touched. Second, the safety might be certain that no defenders are near him, perhaps because the punt was very low or because the punt team was set up for maximum protection while punting from its end zone.

Once the returner has the ball, he should start directly upfield for about three steps. This move draws the attention of the cover people and causes them to adjust their paths inward. The returner then runs in the direction of the return. He must think of getting by the first cover man, either by breaking the tackle or by dodging him.

To signal a fair catch, the receiver must wave his hand overhead. He should be clear in his intention. On occasion, a returner will put his hand up to shield his eyes from the sun and inadvertently signal for a fair catch. Fair catching should also be practiced during the catching period of practice. The returner should make the proper signal, catch the ball, and then drop to one knee with the other knee under the ball. This technique provides extra protection should the ball slip through the returner's hands.

Types of Punt Returns

When returning a punt, the receiving team must hold up the punt team's blockers. For an effective hold-up block, the blocker should get his hands under the opponent's pads to delay his release. If the blocker attacks his opponent on the wall side of the return, it forces the opponent to release to the opposite side of the play.

The return wall should be set wider than the widest man on the line of scrimmage. The wall players should run 10 to 15 yards wider than where the ball was snapped. (Figure 14-1) In a return with two safeties crossing, safety number one knows he will get the ball. If he catches the punt, he fakes the reverse. If safety number two catches the punt, he hands the ball off to safety number one. (Figure 14-2)

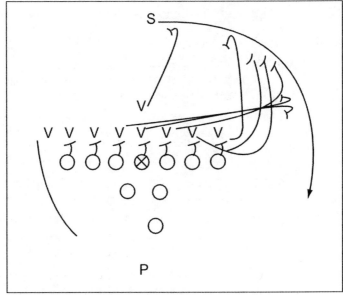

Figure 14-1. A sideline return with a single safety

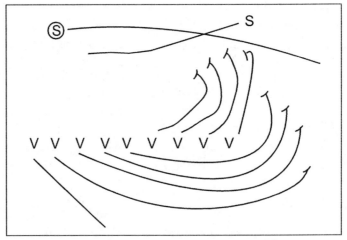

Figure 14-2. A sideline return with a reverse or fake reverse

If the punting team coverage men take wide lanes, the return team may elect to return up the middle. (Figure 14-3) Another type of return starts up the middle, then as one of the defenders is blocked out (trapped), the play breaks outside.

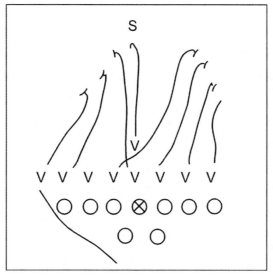

Figure 14-3. Middle return

The punt can be considered a success for the punting team if it nets 35 yards. The punt return team has done its job if the punt nets less than 25 yards.

Punt Blocking

If an opposing team concentrates on punt blocking, the punting team must hold its cover people longer at the line of scrimmage. This situation gives the return team an advantage that can result in a longer return. If the return team rushes four players, then six players are left to set up for the return after fulfilling their first roles, such as hole openers or contain people watching for the fake punt.

Some coaches do not have a great deal of confidence in their personnel, so they don't practice blocking kicks and they don't call for blocks very often during games. Other coaches don't want to risk getting roughing the kicker calls or they simply feel that the negative outcomes outweigh the positive. However, if a coach decides to become more aggressive and develop a punt block mentality, he should start by learning all he can about punt blocking. He should watch tapes of effective punt blocking teams and visit with coaches who have been successful at teaching their teams to block punts. With a new knowledge base, the coach must allocate practice time and start early in spring practice to teach the techniques necessary to block punts. He should identify the players who have the desire to block kicks. The coach can help both the punt blocking unit and the punt team by having them practice together.

By learning the techniques and executing a sound practice plan, the coach will undoubtedly increase the number of punts his team blocks. At the very least, he will force opponents to change their punting schemes. Opposing punt teams will have to hold their cover men longer, their snappers will be under more pressure, and their punters will rush their movements. The impact, therefore, will be much greater than the actual number of blocks.

At the college and pro levels, snappers and punters are highly skilled and protection is very good. At the high school level or lower, however, one or more of these punt team essentials is usually lacking on any team, so more opportunities exist to block kicks.

To assemble and train a good punt blocking unit, the head coach should involve his fastest and most courageous players and dedicate sufficient practice time to preparing the group. The coach should look for punt blockers on the first day of spring practice and tell the team that punt blocking will be emphasized this season. Give every player a chance to block kicks to make everyone understand the difficulty of the task. Tell the team how important punt blocking is to your theory of winning.

To drill punt blocking, assemble several lines of players with a punter 10 yards ahead of each line and off to the side. The blocker runs at the four-yard point. The punter, who can be another player or even a manager, kicks the ball hard enough to travel 15 to 20 yards. A coach stands behind the punter to see if the blocker keeps his eyes open to watch the ball and to see if his hands are extended when the ball is dropped. Many players flinch. If a player can't be trained to see the ball, he will never be a punt blocker. Physical attributes such as speed and height also contribute to good punt blockers, but the primary determination is whether or not he can block punts. Punt blocking is a special talent, so don't send willing but unskilled players to block punts. Use the players who can and will make those blocks.

With a punter at 13 yards and punting from about nine yards behind the line of scrimmage, the blocker has approximately two seconds to run 10 yards. Any player can do that if he is not blocked. Teach punt blockers that their path to the ball should cross in front of the punter so they don't touch him. The scouting report should tell you the exact spot for blockers to attack; this point is typically 4 to 5 yards in front of the punter.

In many cases, the scouting report plays a large part in determining whether or not to attempt to block an opponent's punt. A center who makes slow snaps or is often inaccurate issues an invitation to block his team's punt. A punter who takes too long to deliver the kick or takes more than two steps before kicking is a prime target for a block. Certain situations call for a punt block, such as when a team is behind late in the game or when the opponent is backed up close to its end zone. Coaches should time the other team's punter during pre-game practice and in the game to determine the likelihood a punt block. Coaches should also note how many yards the punter covers with his steps so the punt block spot can be determined with accuracy.

Since the ball usually is kicked from about three to five yards in front of where the kicker started, most punt blockers are told to aim for a spot five yards in front of the kicker's starting point and a foot to his right (if he is right-footed). Some coaches are more cautious and set the spot six yards from the place where the punter started. This tactic reduces the chances of roughing the punter, and the rusher can still adjust to the ball if he has a good chance to block it. In either case, the point is about eight or nine yards behind the center, so punt blockers have 1.8 to 2.2 seconds to run 8 to 12 yards, depending on whether they are rushing from the middle or the end of the defensive line. Two blockers should penetrate the backfield because the personal protector will usually block one of them.

Many teams try simply to bring rushers off the corners for the block, but rushers coming up the middle have a shorter distance to travel. Rushers should watch as the kicker's foot hits the ball and try to put their hands on the ball. They should jump only if they know that their path will take them in front of, and not into, the punter. A rusher coming off the corner has a better chance if he lays out and tries to take the ball off the punter's foot.

It is quicker and easier to block coming up the middle if a teammate can create a hole for the punt rusher. The rusher can get to the block point faster and he does not need to be as close if he is directly in front of the punter.

The 10-man front, which may include one or two linebackers, creates a number of possibilities. Eight gaps exist if there are no split ends, and the snapper need not be counted. In this case, the rush team has four extra rushers. One way to deploy the extra rushers is to overload the outside two or three blockers with four or five rushers. (Figure 14-4)

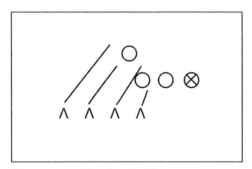

Figure 14-4. Overload of four on two

The simplest alignment for a punt rush is to put someone in each gap with an extra person outside. This alignment can be used on one or both sides of the snapper. A more difficult but often successful method is to create holes for rushers to run through. The hole can be created by down linemen who either charge into a gap and draw a block or actually create a gap with a clubbing or bull-rush action. Coaches should remind players that a hole can be created horizontally by moving the blockers apart, or vertically by driving a blocker backwards. Since most punt teams block passively, often from a two-point stance, an aggressive rush through a lineman may create an opening.

Gaps can also be created on each side of the snapper. The personal protector should pick up one rusher, but the other will come through unblocked.

Another effective formation is the three-man block combination in which the best punt blocker is attacking. Just before the snap, the blocker jumps behind his outside man with his outside leg in the crotch of the outside hole-opener. His inside leg is back and he takes the first step toward the punt block point. The punt block team can use two, three or four down linemen on the offensive blockers. Only two of them know that their job is to open the hole; therefore, the blockers can't key in as to who is opening the hole inward and who is opening it outward. (Figure 14-5)

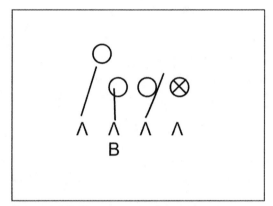

Figure 14-5. Two groups of three on two

It is absolutely essential that all blockers move with the snap. A tenth of a second can make the difference between getting to the blocking point or just missing it. With 1.8 to 2.0 seconds to get to the blocking point, the blocker can't afford to be leisurely about it any more than an Olympic sprinter can be nonchalant about his start in the 100-meter final. That tenth of a second is crucial in both cases.

One method that puts a heavy rush on the middle of the line uses two three-man blocking groups against six offensive blockers. If even a single offensive lineman chooses the wrong man to block, a blocked punt may result. Many coaches always put a defender next to the center to charge the A-gap. The snapper usually is not expected to block effectively anyway, but putting a rusher in his gap may rattle the snapper and increase his chances of making a poor snap. (Figure 14-6)

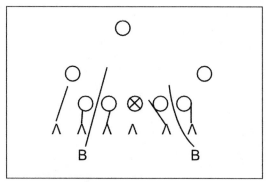

Figure 14-6. Middle rush

Another middle rush loops the nose man around and into the B-gap, which has been cleared. The personal protector may be distracted by an outside rusher and give the nose man a clear rush to the punter. (Figure 14-7)

Figure 14-7. Middle loop

The principles of a good punt block require the rushers to outnumber the blockers at the points of attack, or making the snapper think about a nearby rusher, or knowing where to attack the personal protector. Moving the punt blocking groups at the last second may confuse the blockers in the punt protection. Overloading some areas can leave certain opposing blockers with no one to block and others with too many.

Against a team that uses three-deep personal protectors (sometimes called the three tackles back formation), attack just one of the deep men. This technique renders the other two protectors useless. A rusher might have to come off the corner so the punt blockers are both on the same side of the ball. A coach must also recognize that the three tackles back formation sacrifices coverage for protection, so he should plan for a big return. (Figure 14-8)

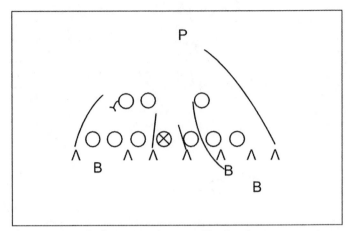

Figure 14-8. Block against three tackles back

As they practice punt blocking, teams should also practice scoring after the block. Once the punt is blocked, there is a clear path to the goal line for a player who picks up the ball and runs. Picking up a bouncing ball while running at full speed is not the easiest of tasks, but there is an effective way to do it: While running at the ball, put one hand under it and scoop it up. This technique is much more effective than reaching down and trying to pick the ball up with both hands. This technique must be practiced, however, because it is not a natural way to pick up a football. Even if the player scoops the ball but can't control it, he still sends it toward the goal line he wants to cross. If the play was a fourth-down punt, the defense gets possession even if a punting team player recovers the ball.

Even with a 10-man block, a chance exists for a return. A punt team often puts extra effort into blocking against a punt blocking team, but this slows down their coverage. Thus, an effective punt blocking team presents a constant threat not only for a block, but also for a good return.

The Partially-blocked Kick

The return team should always get away from a partially-blocked punt that has crossed the line of scrimmage. The word "Peter" is commonly used to warn players to get away from a short kick. A short or partially-blocked punt that crosses the line of scrimmage belongs to the receiving team, so there is no reason for the receivers to touch it. They must have that collective mentality to stay away from it.

Punt Situations to Teach and Practice

• Fair catch rules

• Blocking a punt and covering a blocked punt

- Reacting to a partially blocked punt on your side of the line of scrimmage and beyond the line of scrimmage

- Reacting to a punt you blocked or one of yours that has been blocked

- Scooping up a blocked punt

- Blocking a punt in the end zone

- Receiving a punt deep in your own territory

- Fake punt defense

- Receiving punts (midfield and deep in your territory)

Scouting the Punting Game

Timing the snaps and the punter provides the most valuable information a punt blocking team can learn. If the total kick time is 2.2 seconds or more, then a good chance exists to block the kick. The snapper's accuracy should also be charted. Do rushers bother his snap? Is he responsible for blocking? Does he raise his hips just before the snap to allow punt blockers to get a jump?

Determine the block point for the punt blockers. The punter's steps should help in aiming blockers at a spot about two feet in front of where the ball is dropped on the punter's foot. As a general rule, the aiming point is about four-and-a-half to five yards in front of where the punter stands.

Determine the opponent's punt team alignment and protection rules. Is there a weak link in their blockers? How well do the backs pick up rushers? What are their responsibilities—inside or outside? Will a block work from each side or from an overload on one side?

Check the coverage lanes. Who has contain? Can he be trapped out? Are the lanes close enough together to allow an outside return? Are their lanes wide enough to allow for middle returns? Do they ever fake a punt? What are their punt fake plays?

Rules Relating to a Punt

- Either team can advance a blocked punt if it has not crossed the line of scrimmage.

- If a punt is partially blocked and crosses the line of scrimmage, it belongs to the receiving team unless it is touched by the receivers, in which case it can be recovered by either team.

- A touch by a member of the kicking team does not down the ball; it is live until the official blows his whistle to signal the end of the play.

- If the kicking team wants to down the ball, a player must hold the ball until it is blown dead.

- If the ball is touched by the kicking team, the receivers have the choice of taking the ball at any spot where it was touched or taking the result of the play.

- A fair catch signal only gives the receivers an opportunity to catch the ball. If fumbled, the ball is live and can be recovered by either team.

Drills For Returners

- Catch as many kicks as possible:

- Stand farther back from where the kick is expected, then move into position and set the feet as you prepare to make the catch.

- Stand closer to the kicker than where the ball is expected to land, and run back to catch the kick.

- If a Jugs-type football passing machine is available, use it as often as possible.

- When it is windy, practice catching punts in a crosswind, into the wind, and with the wind.

15

The Kick Scoring Game

The abilities of modern kickers have increased the chances of success of field goals and extra points. About 30 years ago, fewer than 100 successful field goals were kicked each year in major college football. Today, hundreds are kicked every year. The increased length and accuracy of kickers has great ramifications on strategies involving field goals and extra points as well as their defense.

Field Goal and Point After Touchdown

In most cases, coaches use their biggest and best blockers on field goal and extra point plays. The guard can overlap his inside foot behind the snapper's foot. This stance gives him a better inside seal. Neither the tackle nor the end can overlap before the snap, but at the snap he can step behind the foot of the teammate to his inside. Blocking responsibility is always to the inside. Two common types of blocking exist: With the first method, the lineman is taught to step inside, to stay square, to not move his outside foot, and to protect the inside gap. The other method is often called the elephant block because the head of each lineman moves to the hip of the lineman to his inside, so the formation looks similar to a bunch of circus elephants at the finale of their act. The elephant block is simple to teach, however, and it easily seals off the inside. The lineman steps so his inside foot is behind the outside foot of the man to his inside, and he plants his outside foot so a gap is not created to his outside.

Most teams place their wingbacks outside of the ends. Pressure usually comes in this area. The wingback first must bump the inside rusher with his inside hand to throw him off stride, and then bump the outside rusher with his outside hand. (Figure 15-1)

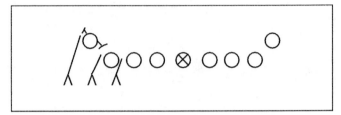

Figure 15-1

Some teams make it easier for the wingbacks by putting them inside or behind the end, which allows them to attack the two or more outside rushers from the inside. By popping the inside rusher first, the wingback may be able to throw the outside rushers off their stride. Once he has prevented an inside rusher from coming inside, the wingback continues to protect the outside by shuffling, basketball-style, in a line parallel to the sideline and directly behind his original alignment. (Figure 15-2)

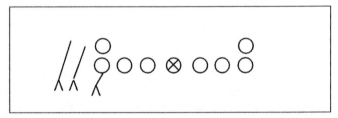

Figure 15-2. Wing back inside-out block

Coaches continue to come up with new and different approaches to many segments of the game. A recent innovation is an unbalanced line to the left side with both wingbacks to the right. This formation still has four blockers on each side, but the right side has three potential receivers. The available three-man pattern offers excellent options for fake or "fire" situations, and it creates potential for two-point play with floods and crossing patterns. When blocking for the kick, the left end works as a wingback, dropping and protecting the inside. (Figure 15-3)

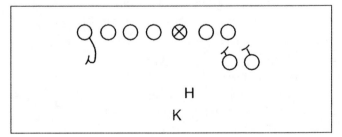

Figure 15-3. Unbalanced with wings on same side

The Spot of the Ball

Most teams place the ball seven yards back for extra points and field goals. On this spot the ball is in the pocket, where it can be effectively protected. Different types of kick blocks may cause a team to change the spot of the ball. The anticipation of tall players coming strong in a middle rush, for example, may force the ball to be spotted about eight yards deep in order to get it over the outstretched hands of tall, penetrating middle rushers and jumpers. The kinds of rushes faced and the kick's trajectory should determine the spot. With long field goal attempts, the ball is easier to block because its trajectory is lower, so these attempts are often taken from a spot deeper than the normal seven yards.

The most important members of the field goal and point after touchdown team are the snapper, the holder and the kicker. Each of these players must be coached long and hard during the off-season, and they need to practice daily during the season. The snapper must get the ball back with speed and accuracy. A good snapper also gets the laces into the holder's hands so he doesn't have to spin the ball. The holder must place the ball when and where the kicker expects it. If the snapper and holder do their jobs properly, then the kick should be automatic. But, if the snap is off-target and delays the hold, or if the hold is not on the expected spot, the kicker has another variable or two to contend with and his chances of success are reduced. The total time for the snap and kick should be 1.4 seconds or less.

With practice the snapper can put the laces where the holder wants them. The following exercise will show the snapper how to hold the ball in order to put the laces in the right position: At the correct kicking distance, have the snapper make several snaps, starting with the laces of the ball facing straight up. Check to see where the laces are when the holder catches the ball. If the laces are exactly facing the kicker, have the snapper snap with the laces straight down. Keep adjusting until the snapper can put the ball where the holder can catch it and place it so the laces point between the uprights. Outstanding snappers can put the laces in the same spot every time as long as the distance to the holder's hands is exactly the same. This precision is developed only through many hours of practice. Skills such as this can easily be learned in the spring and summer. At the high school level, these techniques can be done during the lunch break if there is no other time to learn it. They can even be practiced in the weight room as a station for the snapper and holder.

The snap must be both fast and accurate. Since the kick must be away in 1.3 to 1.4 seconds, the snap should be in the holder's hands in .4 to .5 seconds. Accuracy is more important than speed, however. A fast but high snap, for example, must first be controlled by the holder before it can be placed down, and that step takes additional time. The snap should be low; one foot above the ground is perfect. If possible, the laces should be pointed upward as they hit the holder's hands.

The holder positions himself with his forward knee on the ground. The leg closest to the snapper is flexed. The cleats under the flexed foot should be on the ground so the holder can stand up if necessary to handle a bad snap, or to get up quickly if a fake kick is called. The hand closest to the kicker may touch the tee or teeing spot while the other hand provides a target for the snapper. The holder should become adept at placing the ball exactly on the spot.

As the ball is caught, the holder turns the laces forward so they do not affect the flight of the ball. Laces to the side may make the ball drift in that direction. Laces to the rear may affect the kick if the kicker's foot contacts them, because the laces are a dead spot on the ball. The hold is maintained with one finger of either hand.

The hold should be straight up and down or slightly tilted back. A properly kicked ball will not drift. However, if a soccer-style kicker puts a consistent curve on the ball, it can usually be straightened out by tilting the top of the ball away from the curve. If wind is a factor, the holder can tilt the top of the ball into the wind about an inch to help offset the effect of the wind. If the snap is so bad that it is unplayable, the holder should call "Fire!" to alert the team to execute the predetermined play.

The Placekick

The placekick is used to score extra points, field goals, and to kick off. The older style of placekicking was the straight-ahead kick. This method is quite accurate but lacks the distance of the more popular soccer-style kick. The soccer-style kick allows the player to get a longer leg whip prior to the kick, increased power from hip rotation, and to get more foot into the ball. These three factors combine to impart increased force to the ball to the ball. In addition, since more of the foot contacts the ball, there is more margin for error than with the straight-ahead kicking technique in which a slight misplacement of the kicking toe may misdirect the ball.

The Soccer-style Kick

The soccer-style kick has greater power than the straight-ahead kick and is preferred by major kicking coaches for players who want to kick off long or to kick long field goals. Since the ball is contacted higher and with the thick part of the foot, more power but less rotary motion is imparted to the ball. This combination means the ball does not rise as quickly as a straight-ahead kick.

The kicker must experiment to determine an exact starting point for his stance. Most kickers take three normal steps straight back from the ball, and then take two small steps of about two to two-and-a-half feet each to the side away from the kicking foot. These steps put the kicker at a 30-degree angle to the ball. From this point, the kicker may step up or back another foot in order to get to the precise spot where he feels most comfortable in his approach to the ball.

If a right-footed kicker approaches the ball from greater than a 30-degree angle, the ball will generally slice to the right. If he approaches the ball from less than a 30-degree angle, the kick will generally hook to the left.

Most kickers take a stance with the kicking foot back, which gives them two steps into the kick, but the kicker should use any stance that makes him comfortable. He should keep his head down and his eyes on the target where the ball will be placed.

The kicker starts forward as the ball makes contact with the holder's hands. The kicker may take his first step with either foot and adjust the length of each step to get his kicking foot to the ball at the right instant.

A critical part of the kicking action is the foot plant of the non-kicking leg. Most kickers plant the foot instep-first, and then plant the heel. The kicker must align his plant foot with the desired flight of the ball; his toes should point at the target.

The kicker's plant foot should be six to eight inches to the side of the ball. If he is kicking off grass, the kicker's big toe should be six to eight inches ahead of the ball. If kicking from a one-inch tee, the kicker's big toe should be two to four inches forward of the tee. These instructions are guidelines; a kicker must adjust each aspect of the kick to his own mechanics.

Correct placement of the non-kicking foot is essential for an accurate kick. Right-footed kickers may correct inaccurate kicks by following these foot-planting cues: If the ball hooks left, the plant foot is probably too close to the ball. If the ball slices to the right, the foot plant spot may be too far from the ball. If kicks are too low, then either the planted foot is too far back or the kicker is leaning backward. Since correct placement of the plant foot is so important, it must be practiced frequently. The kicker should adjust the starting point and angle of approach until his foot plant is perfect every time.

The kicking leg swings down through the ball. The kicker should contact the ball about five inches above the bottom tip of the ball, or about an inch to an inch-and-a-half below the middle of the ball. The lower the foot contact on the ball, the more rotary or end-over-end action; this ball action produces a shorter kick.

The toes must be pointed down and the ankle extended throughout the arc of the kicking leg's downward swing. When coaching a kicker, stand several yards in front of him as he makes his approach. Check to see if part of his toes extend past the ball.

The knee extends quickly; the common term applied to this action is "fast knee". To achieve more distance on a kick, the kicker uses the normal approach but whips his leg more quickly. His body must remain forward to obtain maximum power. His eyes must be on the ball. His body must lean forward throughout the kicking action. If the kicker is too upright or if he leans backward, the result will be a low or hooked kick.

The average soccer player kicks with an arcing foot movement, but usually he can be taught to follow through at the target. This adjustment straightens the kick in most cases, and it allows for a more efficient transfer of power.

To get more height when kicking off grass, the kicker should bend the knee on his kicking leg more forward and contact the ball with the outside part of the instep. This "nine iron" effect lifts the ball more quickly than when the ball is contacted with the inside part of the instep.

The follow-through should be straight toward the target. The more the body turns, the greater the chance of error. The follow-through should be high. The shorter the follow-through, the greater the chance that the leg loses power and speed while in contact with the ball. The kicker hops on his non-kicking foot as his body moves through the ball and his leg follows through.

The Straight-ahead Kick

The straight-ahead kick was the exclusive method for kicking the football until the soccer-style kick proved to have more advantages. The straight-ahead kick is seldom used today at higher levels of play; however, because it doesn't have the hooking or arcing trajectory of many soccer-style kicks, it can be more accurate. A straight-ahead kick also tends to get into the air more quickly, so is harder to block. The chief disadvantage of the straight-ahead kick is its lack of distance compared to the soccer-style kick. In a straight-ahead kick, only the toe makes contact with the ball, while a soccer-style kicker strikes the ball with his entire instep and transfers more power to the kick. However, the co-holder of the NFL record for the longest field goal is Tom Dempsey, a straight-ahead kicker who set the record in 1970.

For a straight-ahead kick, the kicker's kicking foot is forward and he bends at the waist. His eyes are on the teeing spot. As the ball hits the holder's hands, the kicker takes a one-foot step with his kicking foot. A longer step can generate more body speed and leg power; it also takes longer, however, so it increases the likelihood of a block or other negative result.

The kicker must continue to focus his eyes on the target as he takes his steps. He takes a long second step with his non-kicking leg as he swings his kicking leg back. The farther back his kicking leg moves, the more power it can generate. The kicker plants his non-kicking foot about four inches outside and 8 to 10 inches behind the ball. The exact distance depends on the height of the tee and the length of the kicker's leg. If kicking from the ground, the planted foot should be six to eight inches behind the ball. If using a one-inch tee, the plant should be seven to nine inches back.

The kicker's target should be one to one-and-a-half inches below the center of the ball. A lower contact point causes the ball to rise more quickly, but it also reduces the distance of the kick because much of the power is spent on rotation of the ball instead of forward motion.

The kicker's thigh comes forward as his abdominal muscles and hip flexors contract. The knee extensors straighten the leg as the ball is kicked. Depending on his leg speed, the toe of the kicker's foot may go as deep as three to four inches into the ball. The ball stays in contact with the toe from the time it is struck until it is 12 to 18 inches off the ground. The greater the leg speed, the longer the ball will remain on the foot.

The ankle must remain locked at a 90-degree angle from the time it starts forward until the follow-through is completed. Some kickers tie a shoelace from the bottom lace to the ankle in order to keep the foot up, but this tactic is not recommended because it requires an adjustment to both the step and the hold.

The foot should remain parallel to the line of the arc of the kicking leg. An error as small as one degree may create a twist of the leg or ankle when the ball is contacted. Such an error may reduce the power and accuracy of the kick. The muscles that control the twist of the thigh and rotation of the ankle must be strong enough to overcome any torque that is created as the foot makes contact with the ball.

The kicker's leg continues up and through the ball and finishes as close as possible to the kicking-side shoulder. After the kick, the kicker will land on his non-kicking foot. The kicker must keep his eye on the ball until he completes the kick. Many coaches teach kickers to keep watching the ground or the tee during the follow-through to make they continue to focus on the target. This is problematic for most kickers, however, because it reduces the ability to follow through completely with the kicking leg and to kick through the ball with the whole body. Following through with the entire body is essential for every kick.

Two-point Conversion from a Placekick Formation

Most teams line up in their basic offense if they need a two-point conversion. However, a scouting report may show coaches that their team has a better chance of scoring from a kicking alignment. If the defense plays man-to-man on the eligible receivers, for example, a crossing pattern could be successful. A high-low pattern might work against one defender covering the flat in a zone. An option with the holder optioning to the kicker might work versus an outside rush with no contain. An option with the kicker running or passing to the off-side end on a drag pattern is another possibility. A formation with two wingbacks on one side also presents a number of passing options.

Field Goal Coverage

Any of the aforementioned formations can be used when kicking a field goal. An unsuccessful field goal attempt can be returned, so coverage must be a concern. The elephants may have to become lions after a block or unsuccessful kick because aggressive kick coverage will be important.

Last-play Field Goal

In a must-win situation, the kicking team is not concerned with coverage because they must execute a successful kick to win the game. Maximum protection against an 11-man rush is all-important. This situation must be practiced so the field goal team develops confidence in its ability to block the all-out rush.

With no time-outs remaining and the clock running, the kicking team must get on the field, set up quickly, and then make the kick. If possible, the quarterback should spike the ball on an early down to stop the clock. With the clock stopped, the field goal unit can avoid a last-second rush to the field that may cause a mistake or produce a penalty.

Fake Field Goal

A scouting report may indicate an opportunity to execute a fake field goal. For instance, the defense may send a safety back for the possible return, thus removing one defender from coverage. The same plays that were covered for fake extra point plays might also be successful for fake field goals. Another possibility in a fake field goal situation has the quarterback roll right and throw a screen back to the left end as the wingback clears.

Free Kick Option in High School

High school rules specify that the receiving team may choose either a first-and-ten or a free kick after a fair catch of a non-kickoff punt. Many coaches are not aware of this rule or the possibilities it presents. The rule gives a team an opportunity to score three points after a fair catch, especially if the ball is caught on the opponent's end of the field.

At the high school level, it is important to practice making a fair catch when the opponent kicks out of its end zone and three points will win the game. After the fair catch, send out the kickoff team, tee the ball up, and make your unblocked field goal. The opponents must line up at least 10 yards away.

Defending the Field Goal or Extra Point Try

The defense should always be ready for a fake field goal or fake extra point because the offensive team can score two points for a run or pass after a touchdown, while only one point can be scored on a kick.

Teams try to block a field goal or extra point either by attempting to collapse the middle of the offensive line or by overloading at the end of the line. The middle block is effective if the team has strong linemen who can collapse the offensive middle and a tall jumper or two who can follow the linemen.

The scouting report is very useful for uncovering the most obvious weaknesses in the offensive blockers. Knowing the upward angle of the kick is also very important. A kick that rises quickly has much less chance of being blocked than a kick with a low trajectory.

Most teams come off the corner for the block. To execute this move, one blocker must occupy the offensive end while a second blocker rushes inside the wingback and a third rushes outside the wingback. The second man should rush close to the tail of the end blocker, starting in an almost flat path and adjusting to a spot a yard in front of the ball placement. His flat path behind the end makes it very difficult for the wing to effectively block him while also blocking the outside rusher. If the first rusher went directly at the blocking target, it would be easier for the wing to make contact with both players. The first rusher must travel about seven yards to get to the blocking point.

The outside rusher takes a path directly to the spot a yard ahead of the ball placement. He must travel about eight yards to the blocking point; therefore, he must be able to run eight yards in 1.3 to 1.5 seconds to be able to block the kick. The outside rusher can shorten the time to the blocking point by diving two to three yards before he gets there. The rusher should dive so that his head and hands are about three feet above the ground as they pass the blocking point. This block should be attempted from only one side or else the two outside rushers may collide head-on. (Figure 15-4) If a weakness can be found in an offensive blocker, use the same hole-opening techniques discussed in Chapter 14 to exploit this weakness.

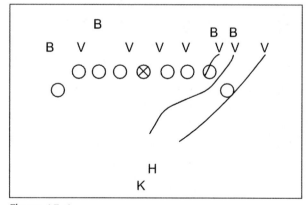

Figure 15-4

Field Goal Return

The longer the field goal attempt, the more important this aspect of the kicking game becomes. The first consideration is whether or not to take the touchback if the ball goes into the end zone. The second consideration is where to set the wall. For most levels of football, it is easier to always use a right-side return. This strategy makes the play easier to practice and execute.

Scouting the Kick Scoring Game

As a coach scouts an opponent's kick scoring game, he should answer the following questions: What is the total kick time? How likely is the snapper to be errant with his snap? How long does it take the holder to get the ball down? What is the trajectory of the ball off the ground? How does the offensive line block? Is there a player who moves his feet and creates a hole we can stunt through? Where is the weakness? A blocked extra point or field goal wins many games for the blocking team. Study the situation. Is there a chance to block the kick? Where and how should you do it?

A coach should also pay attention to how the opponent fakes a field goal, or how he might fake it. The kick defense must be drilled to react to the fake and to the "fire" adjustment on a bad snap. The defense should have at least one contain man on each side, and one or two players must be prepared to defend potential receivers.

Prepare the kick defense for every situation that might occur. For example: At the end of the first half, if your opponent trails by six points or more and lines up for a field goal, be alert for a fake. On the other hand, if you lead by two and your opponent has the ball on your 10-yard for the last play of the game, a field goal attempt is a virtual certainty. An 11-man rush would be appropriate in this situation.

Try to find the weakness in the opponent's protection scheme. If the whole field goal team blocks down, the weakness will be between the end and the wing. If they all block straight ahead, a weakness may exist in the middle.

A blocked field goal that is returned for a score by the defense is seen as a 9- to 11-point play—the three points the kicking team didn't score plus the six to eight points the kick blocking team scored instead. Such a play is a great momentum-builder for the blocking team.

Practice the Special Situations in the Kick Scoring Game

- Poor snap on your point after touchdown (automatic "fire" play for two points)

- Bad snap on the field goal attempt (automatic "fire" play for a first down or touchdown)

- Defending a fake point after touchdown

- Defending a fake field goal

- Returning a short field goal attempt

- Getting the field goal team onto the field with no time-outs

16

Planning and Practicing to Win

Misalignments and missed assignments lose a lot of games. The coach must take a great deal of responsibility for limiting these negatives. He must make sure the players thoroughly understand their assignments and are prepared to handle the impact areas that have been discussed in this book. Careful planning is also involved in order to devote enough practice time to these impact areas prior to the first game and for every game thereafter.

The coach should spend time determining how he wants his team to look. Then, he should list the things he must teach in order to win. He should answer questions such as: What formations, plays and patterns are essential to the offense? Which of these are appropriate for the red zone attack? Do we need another play or two for this critical area? What alignments, coverages, and blitzes are essential for the defense? What kicking and kick receiving plays are essential? The coach must address these issues with his players while emphasizing the impact areas.

A head coach can work his offense or defense in critical third-down situations. The team can work on blitz and blitz pick-up. The coach can make someone responsible for checking encroachment on every play. He will make penalty reduction a part of his meeting and practice work. He will spend time on red zone and goal line offense and defense.

Once the coach has developed his vision and understands it, he must lead his players to understand it. It's not what the coaches know, but what the players know that counts in a game. The coach should not only say "KISS" (Keep It Simple, Stupid), but also practice it. In order to have a sharp alignment and assignment team, the coach must limit the number of schemes taught so the team can come closer to mastering all of them.

A coach who puts six running plays in the playbook might encounter 10 basic defensive alignments against each play. As a result, 60 variables must be practiced. If the coach has 20 plays against 10 different expected defenses, then 200 variables exist. The coach's decision is one of quality versus quantity.

Once the coach decides what he wants his team to do well, he must allot the necessary practice time. Most coaches practice situational football to one degree or another. Professional teams often practice as many as 70 special situations. High school and college teams don't have the time to practice as many situations, but they can practice those situations that are likely to occur weekly. Other situations might present themselves only once or twice per season. Regardless of how often it occurs, each special situation should still be practiced at least once during the season.

Frank Beamer of Virginia Tech has his team cover 33 special situations on the Saturday practice prior to the first game. The special situations include:

- The quarterback has a pass batted back to him. What should he do? Some catch it and run, and they usually lose yardage. In college, the quarterback incurs a penalty if he tries to throw the ball a second time. Therefore, the quarterback should be taught to bat the ball down. (In high school, the quarterback can attempt to throw the ball again.)

- When should a defender knock down a pass instead of trying for the interception? In most cases, on fourth down the defender should knock the ball down and take it at the line of scrimmage. What if a flat pass or a screen can be intercepted? The likelihood of an open field in front of the defender dictates that he should intercept the pass and try to score.

- When the offensive team scores, they should stay on the field until a decision about the conversion is made. If half of the offensive unit leaves the field and the coach decides to go for two, then the time it takes to get them back in the huddle and to the line of scrimmage may result in a penalty. In any case, the lack of organization will reduce the chances for a successful play.

- When a bad snap occurs on a third-down punt or field goal attempt, the holder or kicker should throw the ball toward an upback, and then re-kick on fourth down.

Practicing the Offensive and Defensive Big Plays

The Monday practice is a good time to go over offensive big plays planned for the week and the big plays that must be defended. Players tend to remember the first and last things they hear and do: Practice all the big plays on Monday, scatter some additional practice throughout the week, and then review them at the last practice of the week. This practice strategy should plant the seed deep in their minds.

For the defense, practice against the big plays that can cause problems. These plays include the reverse, the screen, the halfback pass, the onside kick, the hook-and-go, the hook-and-lateral, the out-and-up, bootlegs, counters, and throw-backs.

An opponent might set up a big play in this manner: The offense runs a reverse at some time in the first half, and then runs a fake reverse later in the game, and finally runs the reverse-and-pass for a touchdown. Even when these plays are expected and practiced against, players have a tendency to be lulled to sleep and often become victims of such a strategy. However, preparation is always better than ignoring these tendencies.

If time permits, a coach might prepare his team by practicing against a likely twist on an opponent's series, even if the opponent hasn't tried it up to that point.

Helping the Team Concentrate

Players sometimes jump offside, drop sure interceptions, or fumble the ball. When these mistakes occur in practice, some coaches make the entire team do push-ups to remind the offender that his mistake affects the whole team. Some coaches address only the offending player by taking him out of the scrimmage and having him perform some form of "reminders". If a back fumbles in practice, for example, the coach might instruct the player to recover 25 fumbles after practice. If the player repeats the error, the coach may take him out of the starting line up for the next week. No matter how he chooses to address errors, the coach has the responsibility to increase concentration so costly mistakes are not repeated.

The coach should also review his practice plan and the time spent teaching fundamentals as a possible reason for costly mistakes. If a player hasn't practiced the skills, he can't be blamed if he doesn't have them. If a runner is fumbling, has he been drilled daily on protecting the ball with gauntlet drills, running through the Blaster sled, and having the ball pulled away from him in thud scrimmages? As another example, offensive linemen should be drilled to go on a cadence, while defensive linemen should go on movement. A coach should practice effectively the things that can cause his team to win and eliminate the mistakes that can cause it to lose.

Practicing Your Game Plan to Reduce Missed Assignments

Missed assignments and missed alignments cause teams to lose far more often than mismatches. Coaching has a direct effect on missed assignments. The more the coach adds to his offensive and defensive packages, the more he increases the chances of missed assignments or missed alignments. How close to perfect can a team be with 28 running plays and 15 passes? The temptation exists to add just one more route or just one more option, but more variables mean more mistakes.

Preparing a game plan is like packing for a four-day trip: The temptation is to pack a dozen good-looking sport shirts, six bathing suits, and three pairs of sandals. Will you pack them all, or just what is needed? It is not practical to pack everything; four sport shirts and one pair of sandals is probably sufficient. Whether you are developing a seasonal theory of winning or a game plan for next week, as a coach you must decide whether to practice everything, including all 24 runs and 15 passes, or simply what is needed to win.

On your vacation, you can only wear so much. For your game plan, you can only practice so much. Use five runs to each side and 6 passes. If you need to add another play, you must take something out. If there are too many plays in your game plan, players are much more likely to make mistakes.

As you put together a game plan, think of everything in terms of practice reps. Can your offense block every one of your plays against every defense you expect to see? When will your quarterback audible out of a play because of an unexpected defense? Your team must practice what you expect to use to win. The longer we coach, the more we think of reducing the total scheme; we become more convinced that we don't want any missed assignments.

Think seriously of limiting your game plan. How many runs and passes can your team practice effectively and execute well? Which boots, play actions and dropbacks will you keep for this next game? Which runs offer the best chances for success? Which parts of your kicking game must be perfect and which parts of your opponent's kicking game can you disrupt? Remember to practice the things that can cause you to win and work to eliminate the things that can cause you to lose. Practice scoring and stopping your opponent's scores, every day.

What plays do you expect to use from the 35 to the 20, from the 20 to the 10, from the 10 to the 5, and from the 5 in? The best people should be in the game for every play you want to run. When and how is your opponent likely to blitz? Make sure your team practices it, because if your opponent must stop you, then you surely will see the blitz. What adjustment or play will work best against their blitz? When your team is on defense, when does your opponent stop running vertical pass routes and throw more outs and slants?

How do you want your team to look? Do you really want to win? You want a successful program, so it is essential to make a workable plan, and then to implement it with effective practices. Fundamentals, execution of assignments, motivation, and winning the impact areas are the four keys to success.

About the Authors

Al Groh is the head football coach at the University of Virginia, a position he assumed in December 2000. Previously, he was a member of Bill Parcells' staff from 1989 until he replaced Parcells as head coach of the New York Jets in 2000. As an assistant under Parcells, he served as both linebacker coach and defensive coordinator for the New York Giants and the New England Patriots. Groh has also coached with the Atlanta Falcons, as special teams coordinator and tight end coach; and with the Cleveland Browns, as linebacker coach. He is a former head coach at Wake Forest University and has served as an assistant at The University of South Carolina, Texas Tech, The Air Force Academy, The University of North Carolina, The University of Virginia, and The United States Military Academy. Groh has also served as committee chairman for the Summer Manual of The American Football Coaches Association.

Bob O'Connor is said to have coached at more levels of football than any other member of the American Football Coaches Association, of which he has been a member for more than 40 years. He has coached junior high, high school (as head coach at five different schools), community college, small college, major university, semi-pro, and with two Super Bowl coaches. In his later years, O'Connor has coached the national teams of Australia and Norway and has also coached European football.